MONEY

Myths, truths and alt

Mary Mellor

P

First published in Great Britain in 2019 by

Policy Press
University of Bristol
1-9 Old Park Hill
Bristol
BS2 8BB
UK
t: +44 (0)117 954 5940
pp-info@bristol.ac.uk
www.policypress.co.uk

North America office:
Policy Press
c/o The University of Chicago Press
1427 East 60th Street
Chicago, IL 60637, USA
t: +1 773 702 7700
f: +1 773 702 9756
sales@press.uchicago.edu
www.press.uchicago.edu

British Library Cataloguing in Publication Data
A catalogue record for this book is available from the British Library.

Library of Congress Cataloging-in-Publication Data
A catalog record for this book has been requested.

ISBN 978-1-4473-4627-2 paperback
ISBN 978-1-4473-4629-6 ePub
ISBN 978-1-4473-4630-2 Mobi
ISBN 978-1-4473-4628-9 ePdf

Cover design by Lyn Davies
Printed and bound in Great Britain by TJ International,
Padstow
Policy Press uses environmentally responsible print
partners

What are the 21st century challenges shaping our lives today and in the future? At this time of social, political, economic and cultural disruption, this exciting series, published in association with the British Sociological Association, brings pressing public issues to the general reader, scholars and students. It offers standpoints to shape public conversations and a powerful platform for both scholarly and public debate, proposing better ways of understanding, and living in, our world.

Series Editors: Les Back, Goldsmiths, Pam Cox, University of Essex and Nasar Meer, University of Edinburgh

Other titles in this series:

Published

Miseducation by Diane Reay

Making sense of Brexit by Victor Seidler

Snobbery by David Morgan

What's wrong with work? by Lynne Pettinger

Forthcoming

Cars by Yunis Alam – April 2020

Contents

About the author

Mary Mellor is Emeritus Professor in the Department of Social Sciences at Northumbria University, UK. She has published extensively on gender and the environment, social, green and feminist economics and the democratisation of money as a public resource.

Acknowledgements

Many thanks to all my family and friends for their love and encouragement, particularly Nige, Joe, Kate, Sue, Wendy and Margaret. Also to my colleagues at Northumbria University who have given me unwavering support over many years. Special thanks to Kate McLoughlin for her wonderful cartoons.

Introduction: unlocking the mysteries of money

> Everyone, except an economist, knows what 'money' means.[1]

In the above quote Alison Hingston Quiggin is much too optimistic about the general understanding of money. A more apt quote would be 'not even an economist understands what money means'.

Take a moment to think about the word 'money'. Try to bring an image of money into your mind. Describe that image in the space below before reading further.

Did you envisage a pile of banknotes or a handful of loose change? Did you think of bank vaults full of shiny coins and gold bars? Was the image of your plastic card or your bank account, or money that you owe or don't have? It is not likely that you thought of a notched stick, a string of shells or a tobacco leaf, but these have all been seen as money. Money is one of the most slippery concepts to grasp. It is difficult to define, describe and explain. This is why it seems like magic, a thing of illusion and trickery, mystery and enigma.

Thinking about money is not idle speculation. Money is central to modern life. Lack of access to money can have dire consequences. Earning money is the key focus of most people's lives. Money determines life choices. It dominates political and commercial debate: what is the bottom line? Can these public services be afforded? Despite its importance money retains its mystery. Where does it come from? How does it function?

Conceptions of money influence social and public policy. When challenged that prolonged austerity had forced nurses to rely on food banks, the British prime minister, Theresa May, replied that she could not help because there was no magic money tree. So where *does* money come from? What determines how much money there is and the form it takes? What makes money, money? How is it owned and controlled, or does it exist in some independent dimension of its own?

The book *The Wonderful Wizard of Oz*, captured in the much loved film *The Wizard of Oz*, was written by Frank Baum in 1900 as a parody of the money system. The wizard was believed to be all powerful but behind the curtain it was just a showman pulling strings. In exploring money it is not easy to pull back the curtain. However, it is important to do so, otherwise money will appear to be a naturally occurring, all-powerful phenomenon. If this *was* the case, where is the money mine, the money well or the magic money tree?

If no natural source of money can be found, the conclusion must be that it is something created by human societies. If so, how and when did this happen? If a social source of money cannot be identified, then it does seem to have been created by magic. It has just appeared, out of thin air. There are, of course, many competing explanations of money's origin, form and function, but as we shall see, some are merely fairy tales (see Chapter One and the story in Box 1.1). It is the aim of this book to unlock some of the mysteries about money, challenging various wizards on the way.

Let us return to your image of money. It is quite likely you thought of banknotes and coin. This is the iconic image of modern money as cash. However, this is an illusion because in today's Britain only 3% of total money is made up of notes and coin. The same is true of most globally dominant economies. Many countries are considering going cashless, relying on electronic payments, with Sweden likely to be the first. There is so little physical money because the bulk of money in countries like Britain is held in bank accounts and is mainly transferred directly from one account to another. As we shall see, recognition that bank account records are the equivalent of physical cash is comparatively recent.

If your image was of vaults of gold backing the money you have in your pocket or bank account you will be disappointed. Look at a UK banknote and it says 'I promise to pay the bearer on demand the sum of (twenty, ten, five) pounds'. This is a promise originally made by the Bank of England to exchange notes for gold and it did once hold true, but today the Bank would merely exchange your note for one that is exactly the same. This is described as 'fiat' money.

The word 'fiat' derives from Latin and can be translated as 'let it be done'. Fiat money exists by public authorisation alone. There is no other 'real' money behind it. Most countries do not even make the same seeming promise on their banknotes. The US dollar says 'This note is legal tender for all debts, public and private'. The euro, a much more recent currency, just gives the face-value of the note, five, ten, twenty, fifty euros. It does not feel the need to justify its value either by promising to change it for a superior money or to emphasise that it should be honoured as 'legal tender'. The euro is also unusual in that, unlike most currencies, it has no explicit or implicit backing from a nation-state. However, most currencies are the product of a particular jurisdiction. Pound sterling notes proudly proclaim that they are issued by the Bank of England. The dollar declares it is issued by the Federal Reserve of the United States of America. Euro notes and coins do not indicate who issued them. The peculiar position of the euro will be discussed later in this book.

If your initial image of money was a plastic card or a bank account, or you thought of using your mobile phone to make a money transfer, you are nearer to the reality of modern money. While money exists as base metal coinage, banknotes or records of various sorts, there is no intrinsic value in the medium in which money is represented. Unlike money made of gold or silver, there is no natural limit to the substance of which modern money is composed. There is no shortage of paper to print notes or write cheques or record accounts. There is no shortage of base metal to make coins. There is no shortage of electronic

3

signals to record and transfer data. Unlike the image of a shiny gold coin, modern physical money has no value in itself other than an attraction for numismatists, people who collect coins and notes. The new digital cryptocurrencies take this one stage further by existing only as electronic records. They do not even have an issuing authority. The creation and circulation of the currency is the product of a computer program. As with the euro, the implications of this innovative structure will be discussed later in the book.

What is remarkable about modern money is that, despite the fact that it has no intrinsic value through being made of something valuable in itself like gold or silver, people across the globe use it every day. In fact, in countries that still mainly use notes and coin, notes can become very damaged and fragile, but they still pass from hand to hand. Except in conditions of total self-sufficiency, it would be very difficult to live in most societies without money. Each day trillions upon trillions of transfers of money take place whether as coin, notes, cards, cheques or, increasingly in countries with very few banks, via mobile phones. Markets, shops, businesses of all types, governments, agencies of various sorts, could not function without the circulation of money. People rely on receiving money through earnings and wages, allowances and pensions, gifts, remittances and other transfers. They use this money for a range of purposes, to pay their bills and taxes, buy goods and services, donate to charity or give to friends and family.

Money can be spent, borrowed, saved, invested, gifted, inherited. It is used for illegal activities, stolen and counterfeited. In Britain, where up to one in twenty pound coins was thought to be counterfeit, in 2017 a new pound coin was introduced that was considered harder to fake. Money, itself, is also a major source of investment and speculation. Currency speculation and hedging is a trillion-dollar industry. This has expanded dramatically since fixed exchange rates between national currencies were removed in the early 1970s. Speculation is betting on the constantly shifting values between currencies. Hedging is insuring against adverse currency changes when making trade deals. These activities account for the vast majority of global currency transactions, variously calculated to be

$3–5 trillion dollars a day. Only a small number relate to real trading or holiday spending.

So why do people trust money? What is special about it that makes it so universal in its reach and use? It is surprising that, since it is so ubiquitous in human societies, money has been a largely neglected topic in both sociology and economics. This has allowed money as a phenomenon to be both misrepresented and misunderstood. Myths about money have built up, particularly within economics, which have had major consequences for both the economy and society. It would seem logical that the study of money would be the preserve of economics, but money's ephemeral nature makes it equally important to analyse as a social phenomenon. This is because at the heart of money is social trust. While money has played a vital social and economic role throughout the ages, it has had no fixed form or structure. Although money has taken physical forms such as shells, coins, notes or plastic cards, the 'moneyness' of those objects is not inherent in the shell, metal, paper or plastic itself: it is in the social meaning attached to whatever is socially defined as money.

Unlike most productive and reproductive structures, money does not have an underlying basis in human existence, such as the demands of reproduction or the need to labour to provide food and other sustenance. There is no bio-physical indicator of why human societies should have developed money. Nor did the discovery of gold and silver create the phenomenon of money. Money existed in various forms in earlier eras. This leads to an interesting social conundrum. While money has no 'natural' basis for its existence, it is clearly a vital structure, particularly in contemporary societies. While having no intrinsic value, it has immense social value.

This book therefore starts from seeing money as a social phenomenon that requires a social explanation. It is a vital subject of study because most people in most societies live within a monetary framework. Obtaining the wherewithal to survive depends on the perceived value and dependability of money. In any society a general loss of faith in money would be disastrous. It could lead commerce to grind to a halt, inflation to set in, or to a run on the banks with the possibility of social unrest. The magic of money is its very intangibility, but this is not an image of money that is widely presented. Governments and banks prefer to put forward the notion of 'sound' money. The alternative view of money that sociological studies reveal is therefore counterintuitive. So what is money?

What is money?

It is best to start with what money is not. Money is not defined by the thing it is made of or associated with. It is not money because it is represented by grain, cattle, gold, silver, wood, paper, beads or stone. If this were the case all gold jewellery, cattle or grain would be money. Money can be made from all of these things or none of them; it can merely be a record of money as in a bank account. Perhaps, then, money is defined by the form it takes regardless of the materials from which it is made: gold, silver or base-metal coins with images, numbers and words on them; special paper in the form of currency notes; specially shaped beads or stones. But then anyone could make a coin, print a banknote or shape a bead. Anyone can create numbers on a computer.

As noted earlier, much modern coinage is counterfeit, and the same is true of some banknotes. However, they circulate because people believe them to be the real thing. So that is one important feature of money: it must be trusted and treated as real. People must believe in the magic that the numbers in their bank accounts represent real purchasing power or means of paying their obligations such as tax. The 'moneyness' of money reflects the trust people have in it, not the form and structure of the money itself.

This only raises a further question. On what is that trust based? What is it that is trusted? It is true that if someone receives a gold coin, trust is less important. It is clear that precious-metal money is valuable in itself. The coin could be melted down and sold for its gold content. However, a lump of metal would not be very useful as money. People would not know how much the gold was worth unless it was expressed as a money value (five pounds or ten dollars). When gold and silver was used as money, coins could be weighed to see if the precious metal content was the same as the face-value. However, even if gold and silver coinage were the epitome of 'real' money, that is not relevant to the present day when money is mainly intangible, a number on paper, or on a computer screen or mobile phone.

This brings the issue back to the question of trust. What is it that people trust about money? An important aspect of trust in market societies is that whatever form the money takes, it represents a value (five, ten, twenty dollars) that can be converted into real goods and services (a coffee, shoes, cinema ticket, bus ride). Such flexible 'general-purpose money' can be used for any goods, services or payment. This is a characteristic of modern currencies. There are examples of more limited forms of money, such as temple money or tribute money in indigenous communities, or, more recently, social money limited to particular locations (the Bristol pound, Ithaca Hours). Whether money is general purpose or more limited, an important feature is that it is transferable. People must be willing to accept it in payment on the understanding that they can pass it on to someone else, whether as a settlement of a debt, a gift or in making a purchase.

Transferability is a key feature of money. Whatever it is made of, whatever form it takes, it represents a nominal value that people trust. A dollar note will pass from hand to hand, money numbers will be electronically moved from account to account, but we still trust its value. Many people have seen this as alienating: reducing human relationships to mere numbers. This was the view of one of the earliest writers on money, Georg Simmel (1858–1918). He saw monetary exchange as the purest form of exchange, void of social interaction. Karl Marx (1818–83) saw monetary exchange as the vehicle of market exploitation. Karl Polanyi (1886–1964) saw what he called general-purpose money as the basis of modern market societies. Max Weber (1864–1920) saw money as aiding the rationalisation of society.

While these assumptions have some validity, emphasis on the social nature of money would see it in a very different light. From this alternative perspective, money can be seen as an important expression of social interaction and trust. How alienated from each other can people be, who implicitly trust interactions with strangers based on coins, pieces of paper, bits of stick or numbers on a computer? Arguably, money is the most social of phenomena. Money is a shared recognition of a means of recognising and transferring value. For this shared recognition to exist there must be a monetary community. This could be as limited as tokens in a babysitting circle, or a local currency, or as wide as a national or international currency. At whatever level it exists, money is pure trust, but in modern economies it is shrouded in mist.

The myths of money

A key aim of this book is to puncture the myths that have grown up around money. The main myth about money in modern society is that it is in short supply. This claim implies that there is a limited pool of money for which people and businesses compete. For individuals, this sets the taxpayer against the welfare recipient, and more broadly public expenditure against the private sector. Within the private sector, a shortage of money is seen as a good thing. It is assumed that competition for money means the best firm or individual wins. Conflict is built into this model. 'Hardworking taxpayers' feel resentment against 'welfare scroungers'. Small enterprises feel they are denied adequate credit from banks, as compared with the big players. People express anger at the state for its shortcomings and at big corporations for failing to pay their fair share of taxes.

There is frustration when requests for public expenditure are met by the politically disabling question 'where's the money to come from?'. This goes to the heart of the money myth. It assumes money comes from somewhere. This begs the question, where is that somewhere? Where is this limited pool of money? What form does it take? Is it a natural phenomenon like a gold mine? If so, who owns and controls it? If not, how is the pool constructed, what is it made of? If there is no pool, then the logic is that money comes from nowhere. If that is the case, how does money operate? Again, who controls the 'magic' by which nothing from nowhere becomes something that constrains social, political and economic choices?

Central to the myth of the shortage of money is the confusing fact that money has at times actually been made of precious or useful things: gold, silver, shells, cattle, grain. However, useful things are not necessarily in short supply. Cattle, grain or tobacco leaves could be plentiful, but still be used as money. Today, however, there is no pretence that money is either precious or useful in itself. Money is made of base metal, paper or electronic records. None are in short supply.

What, then, is the basis of the perceived shortage of money? This is a question this book sets out to answer. It will be shown that the claim that money is in short supply is based upon a lot of other myths about money. These myths in turn create further myths about the role of money in society and the possibilities it enables and constrains. Challenging these myths opens up alternative ways of thinking about money and its role in society. What if money was not scarce? What if there is no fixed pool, but a fluid flow of money between people? What if this flow took place in a social and public context as well as the market?

Myths, truths and alternatives

This book aims to identify and puncture myths about money. This is not to imply that myths are a bad thing. Cultural and religious myths are important in human societies, often addressing aspects of the human condition. Parables, fables, legends and fairy tales can entertain and illuminate. However, myths about money are of a different order because they relate to something generally seen as much more concrete. Hard cash, sound money, the bottom line, monetary limits, all imply something tangible with its own logic. How can something so central to the functioning of economies be subject to myth? Isn't this a field that should be more suitable to scientific analysis? That theories about money can be demonstrated to be mythical is part of the magic of money. Money is something that most people use every day, yet grasping its essence is like chasing a chimera.

Because money is so much part of human societies and human history, myths can be challenged by truths based on evidence that undermine the mythical claims. However, while incontrovertible evidence can help to establish a truth, evidence is not always so clear cut and can be challenged. Even if demonstrably true, evidence is also open to interpretation from alternative perspectives. Unlike myths which are based on untruths, different readings of the evidence are open to challenge through critics returning to the source data and engaging in debate. The problem comes where myths influence even the most basic assumptions, leading to particular conclusions, such as that money has naturally determined, rather than socially determined, limits.

This book is written against a climate of opinion that challenges the notion of 'truth'. Unwelcome information is rejected as 'fake news', whether this can be proved to be the case or not. Internet information is at times purposely generated as fake news. Evidence from experts is rejected in favour of alt-facts that people 'feel' to be true. In such a post-truth era, social scientists need to re-evaluate and re-assert the relevance and value of their arguments and evidence. However, social science has long had its own post-truth doubts. Subjective, interpretive and post-structural perspectives have rejected the objectivist assumptions of positivist and empiricist approaches.

Ironically, the case made here, that 'truths' need to be sought in our understanding of money, is challenging the most would-be scientific of the social sciences, economics. Furthermore, in the face of the claims of the alt-right that their assertions have the same status as that resulting from rigorous research, this book rejects the claim that all knowledge has equal status. This is not to claim an absolute notion of truth, but to assert that there is knowledge that is demonstrably more true than other perspectives. Such knowledge will stand up to interrogation.

This book focuses on two main alternative perspectives on money. One is based on a metallist and market view of the origins and evolution of money that will be substantially exposed as myth. In contrast, another perspective on money will be presented that sees money as a social and political construct. This latter perspective builds on the extensive scholarly work and primary research of many people, as well as my own twenty years of work on money. In order not to interrupt the flow of the argument I have not adopted detailed textual referencing, instead I have provided an annotated bibliography. I apologise in advance to anyone who recognises their own unique contribution, and I will aim to acknowledge such a specific contribution in the bibliography. However, for the most part, radical writing on money covers similar critiques of the metallist and market view, although authors' own preferred conclusions and solutions may differ from those presented here.

Structure of the book

The first chapter sets the scene by exploring the key myths about money that the book seeks to challenge. These are presented in the form of a 'fairy tale' that tells a story of money emerging through the market and precious-metal coinage. I will argue that this story about money is largely based on myth or, at best, a partial analysis, reflecting the commercial history of money. The economic assumptions and policies that flow from the fairy tale will be explored and alternative perspectives on the history and nature of money will be introduced. These myths, truths and alternatives will then be explored through the rest of the book.

Far from the fairy story of money's origin in the market, it will be argued that there is not one history of money, there are three: social, political and commercial. These three threads in the history of money are presented in Chapters Two to Four.

The second chapter reflects upon the 'old magic' of money in pre-market, pre-state societies. It presents a social history of money through evidence from pre-market societies that have developed a range of money forms from huge stones to strings of beads. Here, the origin of money is located in various aspects of social relations such as marriage (dowry), conflict (ransom, injury payment) or power (tribute). These early forms of money are often described as 'special purpose' or 'primitive' money. However, I prefer to describe these as customary money, as there are continuing links with the use of money in a public and social context today, such as fines, gifts and tax.

The third chapter draws its theme from the legend of King Midas and the lust of rulers for gold. This sees the history of money as much more about rulers and the sovereign power to create and control money, than about the market. The political history of money is about power: the development and use of money by rulers and ruling elites. While aspects of money and banking emerged in some of the earliest states, the most notable development was the use of precious metal to create coinage. I will argue that money as cash (coinage and later, currency notes) has always been associated with states.

The link between money and conflict in the building of empires and nations will be explored. I will look in particular at the relationship between money and taxation and how this relationship creates a circuit of money based upon state expenditure and subsequent taxation. I will argue that this ongoing circuit of money is ignored by modern conceptions of public finance. Instead, public finance is seen as being dependent on the 'wealth-creating' private sector, leading to a fundamental misunderstanding of how states are funded.

The fourth chapter describes the conjuring trick whereby banks developed a way to create the national currency out of thin air. This history starts not with coinage, but with the commercial development of money in trade. The new form of money was based on networks of debt promises and agreements between traders. While many agreements were verbal and personal, those that were more formal created credit notes drawn on reputable traders and bankers. These began to fulfil the role of money by being passed on in payment. Over time this commercial circuit of money, based on loans and repayment, evolved into a major source of the supply of new money, effectively conjuring money out of fresh air.

The most crucial aspect of the commercial development of money was its interaction with state money. As the commercial notes began to evolve into banknotes and then national currency notes, rulers started to use commercial credit to fund their expenditure. As a result, states lost control of the power to create money. Instead, rulers and the state became indebted to the newly emerging banking sector. This resulted in the build-up of a 'national debt' owed to the banking and financial sector. Political agitation about reducing this debt has in recent times resulted in the development of a 'handbag economics'. This sees states as being like households, having to 'live within their means', justifying austerity. The strength of the ideology of neoliberal handbag economics has been such that its assumptions are only now being challenged and radical thinking is tiptoeing into a defence of public finance and the sovereign right to create money.

The fifth chapter draws its inspiration from the story of the Sorcerer's Apprentice. While the sorcerer is away the apprentice tries out one of the spells, with disastrous consequences. I will argue that the commercial privatisation of the money supply as debt, as explained in the previous chapter, led to the financial crisis of 2007–08 that nearly brought down the Western banking system. I will show how exploitation of the desire of poor Americans to own their own homes led, through a tangle of financial sleights of hand, to the danger that cash machines across Europe and North America would run dry. This led to the sorcerer/state having to step back in order to end the chaos.

This is a critical chapter because it shows how the response of states to the crisis exposed the illusions of neoliberalism. Based on the fairy-tale myths about money described in the first chapter, neoliberalism claimed that the market was the source of all wealth, and therefore all money. States were most emphatically not to 'print money' on their own account. The hypocrisy of this position was exposed when 'quantitative easing' saw central banks rescue the banking sector by creating vast amounts of electronic money and using it to buy up outstanding debt.

The final two chapters explore the possible futures of money. The sixth chapter looks at innovations that aim to create money outside of the structure of nation-states, most notably, the euro and cryptocurrencies. Both aim to be a technical solution to the need for money by providing a neutral medium of exchange. The euro sought to remove itself from any political authority and act as a resource solely for the commercial sector. Cryptocurrencies go further and aim to exist without any overarching structure. The chapter will argue that both are deeply problematic because they misunderstand the social and political nature of money.

At the other end of the spectrum are the many attempts to set up citizen-organised currencies. These stress the social nature of money and see local, self-organised currencies as building sustainability and solidarity. The weakness of this approach is the lack of a political and commercial framework. Social currencies have so far failed to mount a substantial challenge to either the public currency or the commercial market.

The final chapter seeks to break the spell of conventional economics that obscures the existence of public money, that is, the sovereign power to create public currencies. I will argue that modern public currencies can be understood only if money is seen as having social, public and commercial origins. The case for seeing modern money as social and public, rather than purely instrumental and economic, is its reliance on trust and monetary identity. Money has no intrinsic value, but different monetary communities recognise and acknowledge their own monetary symbols: pounds, euros, yen, dollars. The critical question then becomes, how does that money get into circulation? Where is the magic money tree?

Is there a magic money tree?

Kate Mc

Based on the discussion in Chapters Three and Four, the final chapter will identify two interacting circuits of money: the banking model of debt and repayment and the state model of spending and taxation. I will argue that both circuits exist in modern economies and both must be open to democratic scrutiny. Money is a vital public resource and therefore should be responsive to democratically expressed priorities. Access to money must also be seen as a democratic right. How this could be done will be explored, such as proposals for a basic income, public banks and participatory budgeting. I will argue that the sovereign power to create money needs to be rescued from the commercial banking sector and put in the service of the people. However, this cannot be achieved while myths about money remain in place.

Radical approaches to money are subject to the common criticism that increasing the supply of money, particularly through public spending, would necessarily be inflationary, leading to higher prices in the market-place. This chapter addresses that criticism through a radical reconception of the role of taxation.

What is important about money is that it is a key institution in human societies. It has existed in some form almost everywhere. Yet it is very hard to grasp, like a spectre it slips away, shrouded in mystery. It is a shape-shifter that presents in many different ways. It connects people like an invisible thread. It is the vital link between market and state. It is valued without being valuable. It is a social construct that can be both tangible and intangible. It can be seen as an alienating and exploiting mechanism and as a force for social justice. Challenging myths about money at one level destroys the magic, but opens up its radical potential. However, myths have consequences as will be discussed in the next chapter.

ONE

A fairy tale about money: myths and their consequences

Box 1.1: Fairy-tale economics

Kate Mc

Once upon a time people lived in societies without money. Nevertheless everyone was busy. The hat-maker made hats, the boot-maker made boots, the candle-maker made candles. What they enjoyed most of all was to haggle and barter. Boots were exchanged for candles and hats for boots. The problem was that often the candle-maker did not need boots and the boot-maker did not need a hat. Because of this problem people had to travel far and wide to find a suitable swap.

One morning the hat-maker woke up wearing a wizard's hat. Inside the hat was a great idea. Why didn't everybody exchange for something they all desired? What everybody in that land desired was gold and other precious metals. These metals were also very useful as they were easy to break down into smaller pieces and they could be made into different shapes. Gold was particularly valued as it did not corrode. Everyone was delighted and the number of exchanges increased dramatically. The hat-maker sold her hats for gold and then used the gold to buy gloves. The glove-maker then used the gold to buy a winter coat and the coat-maker used the gold to buy boots. In this way the gold continued to pass from hand to hand.

The trouble was that there were brigands in the land who also loved gold and silver. People were frightened of carrying the gold on their travels or having a pile of gold in their homes in case it was stolen. The solution came from special people who worked with gold and silver. They had to have strong, safe places to keep the metal and were called bankers because, in Italy, where they first appeared, they sat on a bench to do their work (*banco* is old Italian for bench or table). So the traders left their gold and silver with the bankers.

The bankers then had a bright idea of their own. Some people seemed to have lots of gold and silver and others didn't have any. The solution was that those people who had lots would lend to those who didn't have any. The bankers would arrange everything and take a fee for doing so. They also had a solution to the problem of carrying gold around. Why didn't people just carry a record of their deposits of gold and silver certified by the banker? Instead of actually handing over the metal when trading, people handed over the certificate issued by the bank. Because the bank was trusted to really have that metal, the notes recording deposits passed readily from hand to hand.

As a result, lots of people had notes of different amounts relating to a range of deposits of precious metal. The bankers had a solution to this also. They would gather up all these notes and calculate who owed what to whom. As the notes tended to cancel each other out, at the end of each accounting period only a relatively small amount of metal needed to change hands. The bankers would then transfer that precious metal between the relevant deposits. This process was known as clearing. It was magic because huge numbers of paper exchanges boiled down to a much smaller actual transfer of metal.

Realising that people did not generally want to use their metal deposits in their trading activities, the bankers saw a new way of making money for themselves. They issued far more notes that promised access to the metal than they had metal. They then lent those notes to people who didn't have any metal themselves, or not enough for the trading they wanted to do. The borrowers promised to return the notes at an agreed date with interest. This innovation required some new magic because if everyone wanted metal in exchange for the paper notes at the same time, the bank would run out of metal very quickly. The bankers consulted a money wizard who cast a spell that made everyone trust the paper money. However, sometimes the spell failed and people began to rush to the bank to make sure their metal money was still there. Something was needed to make people feel comfortable about the imbalance between paper money and metal money.

As it happened, the money wizard had travelled forward in time and seen a film of Frank Baum's, *The Wonderful Wizard of Oz*. The money wizard was impressed by how the film's Wizard of Oz made people feel good. The Wizard of Oz didn't really have magical powers but he made a cowardly lion feel brave by giving him a medal. He made a scarecrow become brainy by awarding him a diploma. He made a tin man emotional by giving him a ticking watch in the shape of a heart. The fairy tale's money wizard said that the banking dilemma could be legitimised with a new concept, 'fractional reserve banking'. So the banks continued to make promises they couldn't keep and everyone lived happily ever after.

Prior to the development of capitalist societies, many people relied on barter – the exchange of one good or service for another.[1]

As the 2017 text-book quotation above shows, the fairy tale in Box 1.1 expresses a story that is still very current in economic thinking: the historical emergence of money from an economy based on barter. The tale also contains a distillation of other key ideas that underlie much of conventional economic and political thinking. The mixture of myths and truths about money that the fairy tale reveals, and the way they are interpreted, is reflected in economic and political decision making. What, then, are the myths and truths about the origin of money revealed in the fairy tale?

Myths and truths about money

The main myth in the fairy tale is about the origin of money in barter. The story tells us that before the invention of money people swapped goods and services directly. This assumes that the two parties each have something the other desires, what economists call 'a coincidence of wants'. Barter also implies a negotiation. The boot-maker and the hat-maker have to come to some agreement about the relative values of boots and hats. Finding someone to directly swap with and settling the relative values is difficult to achieve. The invention of money is a brilliant solution. It provides an independent yardstick by which to determine the relative value of hats and boots and a medium of exchange to save having to find a direct swap. These are the two main functions of money that economists identify.

The only problem is that there is no truth in the fairy tale. Historical and anthropological studies have not found economies based upon barter, certainly not the type of individual barter described in the story. As the next chapter will show, forms of money did exist before the large-scale development of markets, but they were not generally used for the exchange of produce. The myth of money's origin in barter has led to another myth, that money originated in market exchange. Money was certainly used by traders, but forms of money that acted as a yardstick and enabled the transfer of goods and services existed thousands of years before markets were widespread. The invention of coinage, the form of money assumed in the fairy tale, took place two thousand years before market economies became the norm.

The long history of money also challenges the role of precious metal in the origin of money. It is true that precious metal has been used to make forms of money, particularly coinage, but it is not the only form of money, nor the original form of money. What is true is that precious-metal money played an important role in Europe, although, even then, it was symbolic rather than practical. Coinage is also misleading because it survives over time, whereas other forms of money are more transient.

Another area where there is a mixture of truth and myth is the origin of modern banking. The fairy tale sees banking emerging to deal with the insecurity of holding precious-metal money, with the possibility of theft always present. To avoid theft the money is placed with bankers for safe keeping. In its place the owner is given a record of the amount deposited. Because everyone trusts the bankers, the paper record of the deposit acts as money.

It is certainly true that some precious metals were deposited by some traders, but this was not the origin of banking. Like the origin of money, banking is much older than precious-metal money. Forms of banking are traced to the collection and allocation of grain in the early civilisations. Nor did modern banking derive from the invention of precious-metal coin. As will be explained in Chapter Four, the banks of today had their origin in trading agreements and making and guaranteeing loans that were mainly based on paper records.

It is important to challenge these myths and interpretations about the origin of money in barter and the market, the role of precious-metal money and the role of banking, as they have had a major impact on the way money is perceived today. This challenge is important because the myths have social, political and economic consequences.

The myth of barter

The myth of barter is critical to the way modern money is conceived. The idea of barter directly links the existence of money, particularly coinage, to market activities. An early connection between precious-metal money and the urge to trade and profit was put forward by Aristotle (384 BCE –322 BCE). However, he saw the link as something to regret, drawing a distinction between oikonomia and chrematistics. *Oikonomia* roughly translates as 'of the household' and refers to the main form of production in Aristotle's day, subsistence production in the family. It is also the root of the word economics.

However, for Aristotle oikonomia had nothing to do with trade and profit-seeking. He scorns the search for money and wealth as chrematistics (derived from *khrema*, the Greek word for money, and defined as the study of wealth and money). Praise for the activities of 'huckstering and bartering' in the market beloved of Adam Smith (1723–90) had to wait for two thousand years. Even Smith had reservations about economics in the raw, and saw the market as framed in social values based on 'moral sentiments'.

A leading exponent of the idea that money originated in the market was the Austrian economist Carl Menger (1840–1921). He built on the work of Adam Smith to develop the theory that money emerged spontaneously from an earlier form of economy, the era of barter. This story was put forward by Menger in the early 1890s,[2] and since then the myth of barter has become a core idea in conventional economics and, as we have seen, is still repeated in economics text-books. Given that there is no historical evidence of barter economies or even individual bartering on any scale, how did this myth become so pervasive? The answer is that the assertion of the existence of barter is not derived from historical evidence, but from a theory of how money functions in the market.

The myth of barter is the result of a thought experiment. Instead of exploring empirically what type of economy preceded the market, the theory works backwards from the experience of how money operates in market economies. The question then becomes how would markets operate if money had not been invented? The conclusion is that people would barter. The inconvenience of barter would then lead to the invention of money. As the original form of money is assumed to be gold or silver, a 'commodity theory' of the origin of money is born. As the fairy story says, one commodity, precious metal, available on the market, became adopted as money.

Apart from the lack of historical confirmation of this theory, the weakness of the model is the assumption that the same model of market exchange would exist in the earlier era and the only thing that was different was the non-existence of money. This is wrong on two counts. As discussed in the next chapter, most human societies have had some form of money even though they had no markets, and there is no historical evidence of the existence of markets that did not have some form of money.

The myth of barter has profound ideological ramifications. By projecting individualistic market-like behaviour back into pre-market societies, it asserts that market behaviour is a defining aspect of human beings. The emphasis on barter portrays people as individual economic calculators, weighing up the 'utility' of their activities. The associated claim that money originated in the market underpins the current neoliberal ideology of market dominance. Seeing the origin of money in the use of precious-metal coin in market exchange leads to the assumption that the creation and circulation of money must begin and end in the market-place. As wealth is identified with the accumulation of money and assets purchased with money, the market is seen as the ultimate source of wealth, as it 'makes' money.

Seeing the market as the source of money and wealth has had implications for contemporary attitudes to the state. Neoliberal ideology has adopted what I have called a handbag economics that espouses a feminised view of the state. The state is portrayed as a dependent household that must live on whatever 'house-keeping allowance' the market can afford. The less regulation and tax, the smaller the state and the more limits on welfare payments, the better. Money is seen as a scarce and limited resource. If the state spends money this must mean that someone else, the 'hard-pressed taxpayer', must be out of pocket. The only solution must be to cut public expenditure to the bone to leave as much money as possible free for the market if wealth is to be maximised.

Making the provision of goods and services that enable human flourishing dependent on market success has had a devastating impact on social priorities. If there is no other aim than the maximisation of money and wealth that Aristotle criticised, it is unlikely that other considerations such as the well-being of the wider community beyond the market or the preservation of the environment will be achieved.

Far from the myth of a market origin of money, states have played a major role in the history of money, as will be seen in Chapter Three. Most states still have the monopoly of printing banknotes and minting coin. In the latter part of the twentieth and early twenty-first centuries, however, the sovereign power of states to create money was curtailed in the leading market economies by making central banks independent of governments, while at the same time demanding that states should not 'print money'. The latter injunction was rapidly revoked when the Western banking system went into crisis in 2007–08, as will be demonstrated in Chapter Five. I will argue that the continuing role of the state in the creation and circulation of money fundamentally undermines the neoliberal emphasis on the centrality of the market.

The myth of gold

The myth of gold and other precious metals is that they are the original form of money. This is not true. However, what is true is that gold and silver money has played an important role in European culture and this has had a lasting legacy for the way money is perceived. The importance of gold or silver money for the fairy tale is that the precious–metal money has its own intrinsic value. It has this intrinsic value because it is traded as a commodity in the market-place. This means that when people accept the money in exchange for a good or a service they are exchanging items of equal value. When the hat-maker sells her hats, she receives the equivalent value of the hat in gold or silver coin. It is this equivalence in value that is seen as the reason people use and trust money. Gold and silver money has therefore been seen as the ideal, with all more mundane forms of money as a poor reflection.

It is true that many money forms have been valued in themselves. Gold, silver and other precious metals are valued because they are comparatively rare and difficult to access. Similarly, shells which are common in one part of the world may be rare in another part. Other forms of money are useful in themselves rather than rare, such as cattle, grain or tools. Some money is valued because of the level of creativity involved, such as strings of shaped shells, specially woven cloths or carved stone discs. These useful or decorative forms of money are mostly found in pre-market, pre-state societies. However, not all forms of money are rare, useful or beautiful, so none of these attributes is a sufficient explanation of why people trust and use money. They are certainly not true of money today.

The intrinsic value of the precious-metal money in the fairy tale is not based on rarity, use or creativity as such, but on the value of gold or silver metal in the market-place. This is why precious-metal money is often described as commodity money or as *specie* (Latin for 'in kind'). The problem with using a valued commodity as money is how is the precious metal itself to be valued? In a market system, the price of a commodity is determined by the market itself. In that case, for each use of the precious-metal money, its price would need to be negotiated. Precious-metal money could still act as a medium between other goods, but it could not act as a universal measure of value as it, itself, would have no fixed value. Using commodity money is really just another form of barter, haggling between two commodities, the precious metal and whatever good, service or debt is being traded.

This creates a paradox. If the precious metal is to act as money it needs to have a fixed value if one good or service is to be compared with another. However, as a commodity its value must be set by the market. To judge the value of any commodity on the market, a means of measuring comparative values needs to be set. That is the job of money. Gold and silver as commodities cannot be monetary yardsticks for themselves. Commodities cannot determine their relative value without some external standard. One way of dealing with this problem was to price gold and silver against each other, but even then the value of one or other needed to be fixed.

Money having its own intrinsic value creates other problems. What makes the precious-metal money valuable can conflict with its use as money. If the value of money is based on scarcity, there may not be enough money in circulation to enable the full range of market activity. The high value of the coinage may also make it less useful in practice as it could be inappropriate for daily mundane exchanges. Historically, even the smallest precious-metal coins had quite high value, equivalent to several sheep or many days' labour. This made them unsuitable for local small-scale trading such as between the butcher, the baker and the candlestick-maker.

Metals like gold and silver were also not practical because they were very soft and were easily damaged. Coins were open to being 'shaved' by unscrupulous users. Both these problems were solved by mixing precious metal with stronger metals, but that only made the measurement of the value of the coin more difficult. As will be discussed later, the most useful forms of money are those with no value in themselves, the most notable being modern fiat money, which has fixed face-values (ten dollars, five euros, twenty pounds).

If the fairy tale were true and money had emerged spontaneously from commodities such as gold and silver, there would need to be some indication of the historical mechanisms involved. Where did the precious metals come from? Who owned and controlled the mines where they were found? Did the metal start being used as lumps or did it only emerge as coins? Who owned and controlled the minting process? If precious metal was invented as money, there must be a historical moment when the eureka light bulb lit up. Who and where was that? All these questions are neither asked nor answered by the fairy story. The historical evidence does indicate where and when precious metal was mined and invented, but this was long before the era of markets.

Despite the mythical nature of precious-metal money, it had a major impact on European money systems. The main legacy of the fairy tale is that money is thought of as being scarce and valuable, despite the evidence to the contrary. While today it is accepted that the money form does not have its own value, there is a lingering notion that it should be 'backed' by gold or some equivalent. In Britain this idea was actively pursued. As will be discussed in Chapter Three, successive governments imposed a gold standard with the aim of grounding all money in precious metal. This proved to be problematic and the gold standard was frequently suspended and eventually abandoned. Even so, a remnant of the fiction that money is rooted in precious metal still appears on UK banknotes. Each note states 'I promise to pay the bearer on demand the sum of five (or ten, twenty, fifty) pounds', signed by the Chief Cashier of the Bank of England. Originally this was a promise to pay the bearer in metal coin. Today the note would be exchanged for exactly the same note.

And, as pointed out earlier, other modern banknotes make no such promise.

Even if precious metal were the origin of money, it has not been in general circulation in Europe for hundreds of years. It is accepted that all money is now fiat money. That is, valueless in itself, with no backing of any sort of 'real' money that has intrinsic value such as gold. This appears to make modern money no less useful. The fact that today most money exists only as bank records refutes the argument that money should be made of something rare, or of any *thing* at all. There is no natural shortage of bank accounts or banknotes. Any limitation on access to banks, bank loans or banknotes is made by the banks themselves and/or monetary authorities.

The myth of banking

The myths about banking are perhaps the most misleading of all, and those myths are still very much with us. The myths are that money created and circulated by banks should be backed by a reserve (a store of money) or capital assets (the wealth of the bank itself), even if those reserves and assets are 'fractional'. That is, they could only provide a small fraction of the total value of all the accounts registered with the bank (usually a maximum of 10%, often much less). The second myth contradicts the first, that banks are just intermediaries linking savers with borrowers; that is, they have no role in money creation.

In the fairy tale the people took the precious-metal money and placed it in a bank for safe keeping. There is some truth in this. Travelling with precious metal was particularly dangerous. Avoiding these dangers did contribute to the development of paper money and banking. However, this was in the context of long-distance trading or imperial adventures rather than the everyday world of local production and consumption. Despite this, the story assumes that precious metal is used widely in market exchange and deposited in banks. Depositors received a paper record of the amount which they could transfer to someone else in payment. The new holder of the paper could then retrieve all or part of the precious-metal money from the bank.

The story goes on to show how the banking system develops as the deposits become the basis for loans. There are several assumptions about how the loans are made, many of which have resonance today. One is to see the bank acting as a mediator between the depositors and the borrowers. Presumably with their permission. If those deposits are of precious metal or any other limited physical money the depositor-lenders will not be able to retrieve the money borrowed until it has been repaid. Another version is that the bankers do not ask depositors permission, they pool all the deposits and lend them out on the off-chance that not all the depositors will come back at the same time to collect their money. This is the principle of fractional reserve banking.

The approach to lending in the fairy story does not envisage lending out the actual precious-metal deposits, but lending paper entitlements to the money. This allows many more loans to be made, as the money is not physically removed. However, this does not solve the problem, as the fairy tale has to deal with the fact that there is much more paper money in circulation than precious-metal deposits.

An alternative approach to the origin of banking removes the need to have a theory of a 'fractional reserve'. The problem is seen as lying in the association of money with precious metal. This leads to a distinction between 'real' money, the precious metal, and paper 'pretend' money. As discussed in the case of gold above, if precious metal is seen as the ideal of money, paper and other forms of money will always be seen as an inferior version. The scarce and valuable 'reserve' or other form of 'backing' must necessarily be limited. If, however, the paper is seen as money in its own right, the distinction between real and pretend money breaks down.

The myth of the need for reserve deposits of some form of 'real' money persisted until very recent times. It is only with the advent of purely fiat money that some countries, most notably Britain and Canada, realised that the idea of a reserve was meaningless. All the money in circulation could never be paid out in gold or any other 'real' money. Money itself had dematerialised. All that was left was confidence that its notional value (ten dollars, twenty pounds, fifty euros) would be honoured by those to whom it was presented. However, there is still an assumption that bank-created money is 'backed' by the wealth of the bank. Bank regulators call for commercial banks to have 'capital adequacy', with much the same fractional ratios as was the case for reserves. This does not solve the problem, as the amount of money needed in circulation to run a modern economy is much bigger than the available capital assets of banks.

The creation of more circulating money than precious metal or the private wealth of bankers could sustain was essential for the growth of markets and capitalism. The growth in paper money associated with early capitalist trading did not originate in, and was not related to, deposits of precious metal or the actual wealth of individuals. Instead, it represented networks of agreements and promises between traders. The circulating paper was a pattern of debts and credits – that is, a promise to pay back or pay out. Unlike the theory of precious-metal deposits being lent out, the paper promises circulating were just that, promises to pay. The notes were backed by patterns of trust, that credits and debts would be honoured. The word 'credit' comes from the Latin for 'I believe'. This leads to a very different view of what a bank does. Banks are not passive administrators of deposits, they are at the heart of a network of promises.

The fairy-tale myth that banks lend 'funny' money dependent on 'real' deposits is still widely held. This, despite the fact that no one's bank account is raided when banks make a loan. An alternative view, only recently widely accepted, is that in banking loans come first. As will be explained in Chapter Four, deposits do not create loans, loans create deposits. Banks do not base their activities on prior deposits. They create and circulate new money by creating new deposits, every time they make a loan. The circulation of paper notes and bank account transfers *is* the money, not some residual reserves of gold ingots. This is particularly true of modern economies. This raises questions about the privilege commercial banks have to create and circulate new money while this is denied to the public state, which must not 'print money'. The case for democratising the creation and circulation of money will be made in Chapter Seven.

Having explored the myths of money and some of their consequences it is necessary to turn now to look at alternative ways of understanding money.

Untangling the magic: understanding money

The problem in understanding money is that it exists in many contexts and many forms with many uses. A modern dollar is very different from a gold coin or a string of wampum beads. Modern money circulates in an impersonal way, one US dollar is exactly the same as any other US dollar. They look the same and have the same face-value. By contrast, two similar examples of stone money in the Yap economy have different values depending on who owned them and their aesthetic quality, as described in the next chapter.

Most economic text-books explore money by identifying its key functions within a market economy. These are generally given as: a medium of exchange, a unit of account, a means of payment and a store of value. According to the fairy story, money as a medium of exchange is the primary function because it is the origin of money. However, the theory of the adoption of commodity money or specie, even if it were true, has been overtaken by representations of money that have no value in themselves. Today's money is base coin, paper notes, electronic signals. How are we to understand this money and its origin? If money did not originate in the market-place, in what other contexts should it be explored? In the next two chapters I will look at the social and political histories of money; here I will look at some of the key features of money.

Money as a means of transfer

As later chapters will show, while money is certainly used to transfer value in commercial activities, money can also be transferred in many other ways. The definition of money as a medium of exchange implies a direct exchange of money for a good or service, as the idea of barter implies. While this is one use of money, money is used in a wide range of other contexts, private, social and public. Money can be transferred in a one-way direction, as a gift, a fine or a tax payment. It would therefore be more correct to describe money as a medium of transfer rather than specifically a medium of exchange. What, then, is being transferred? While commodity money could enable a direct transfer of value, most money is only a representation of value. It is a promise of value. The promise is that it can be used to purchase goods and services, to pay fines or fees, to pay off debts, to pay taxes or give gifts.

What matters is that people recognise and accept those promises. The beginning of a definition could be that anything is money that people generally accept as a means of calculating and transferring the promise of commercial, social or public value. Money systems can be anything from as extensive as the global use of the US dollar, to national currencies such as the Japanese yen, to local currencies such as the Bristol pound, or the use of tokens in a babysitting circle. The actual money thing that represents the transfer of the promise could be a piece of paper, a sack of grain, a tobacco leaf or an electronic message. In prisons cigarettes are often used as currency. A recipient could use a cigarette as a consumer item and smoke it, or store the cigarette for future transfer. In the first case it is not money, in the second case it is. The cigarette itself does not embody the essence of money, but it can have the essence thrust upon it.

What makes the money-ness of money is not the particular thing, but the level of acceptability or authority of the promise it represents. If we were involved in direct exchange I would do your washing and you would do mine. Payment is complete, all the washing is done. If I give you money for doing my washing, this is a promise that you can spend or transfer it in some other way. In turn, the future recipient of that money can use the transferred promise in various ways. The interesting question is, who has the right to start a chain of promises and how will it end? Logically, money must start somewhere. If money is a chain of transferable promises, some person or institution must have made the first promise. At the end of the process will someone hold a promise that will never be fulfilled? Where do the promises start and where do they end? Is there ever a final payment when the circuit of money ends, or is there just a continuous transfer of promises? I will argue that there are two originating sources of generally recognised transferable promises, which could be described as magic money trees: bank lending and state spending.

Whatever its source, the evidence indicates that money is something valued not for its own sake, but for what it represents. This is the case even when the objects concerned do have intrinsic value. Strings of shells are certainly valued in themselves, but if they were not used as money they would just be ornaments. For example, in India, gold is mainly held as jewellery. Precious objects do act as a store of value, as is the case with Indian gold, but to function as money they have to be presented in a recognisable money form. Gold jewellery must be valued in rupees and if it is to act as money it needs to be minted into coin or sold for the national currency. Commodity money can certainly act as a store of value, but this value is not fixed. Gold and silver fluctuates in price on the market. Similarly, non-precious currencies can have a price which can wildly fluctuate as the cryptocurrency bitcoin did in 2017.

Currencies also have a value in relation to other currencies, bitcoin in terms of dollars or pounds, pounds in relation to euros. However, within a currency the value of the currency is nominal; this means a dollar is worth a dollar. A pound worth a pound. A five pound note is not suddenly worth six pounds. What the five pounds can purchase may vary, but the five pounds itself stays the same. This is the important feature of money. It is the nominal yardstick by which other values are judged.

The magic wand: money as a yardstick

I would argue that, far from being something of value in itself, money is most useful when it has no intrinsic value. Although there are severe political problems with the euro, as will be discussed in Chapter Six, it is very simple as a yardstick of value with its face-value as coin and five, ten, twenty, fifty notes. There is no implication that it relates to any other value. In this it is like a ruler with fixed points. This says nothing about the euro's purchasing power, which can vary widely across communities. This need to have a recognised standard against which to compare values appears to be important for all human societies, regardless of the form money takes, or its usage.

As will be seen in the next chapter, one of the earliest uses of money is as a representation of comparative value. Tributes, gifts, dowries, injury payments are all subject to decisions about the appropriate level expressed in the customary forms of money-thing, be it pigs, teeth, clothes or stones. Gifts can be compared, misdemeanours fined according to severity.

Standards of measurement were important in early civilisations. Institutions such as temples and palaces kept records of the production and allocation of grain and other products. Numbers and weights of grain were commonly used, but a varied range of yardsticks were chosen. One early method of measurement was quite literally a yardstick. The sticks would have standard gaps between notches for different quantities or for other records, such as number of days. Neither sticks nor grain were in short supply, indicating that it was not the money-thing chosen that mattered, as long as it was recognised and consistent. What was important was to have a standard measure that could be used for calculation, comparison and record. This could be used to record incomings and outgoings, calculate yields of grain, compare payments of taxes or allocate food and other items. These records and accounts would be confusing if the value of the standard itself varied. So, unlike the fairy tale of money where people trust the money thing because it is made of a valuable commodity, it is the reliable, standard nature of the chosen money that is most important.

As pointed out earlier, money as a unit of account is exemplified by modern fiat money. Modern money is purely a representation of a social and political promise. There is no intrinsic value in it or behind it. Money can be a coin, a note, a plastic card or a number on a phone. What it says is that the holder is entitled to ask for goods and services to the stated value of the representation or is liable to pay that amount. Money is used to indicate different levels of entitlements (wages, benefits, prizes) and obligations (debts, fines, taxes) which may be social, political or economic.

Having a money with its own value, far from being the origin of money as the fairy tale states, can cause confusion as to whether specie money is a commodity or a money. Money having its own value undermines its function as a unit of account, as there will be no stability over time and across contexts. For this reason, far from being the ideal form of money, specie money is arguably the least ideal.

Challenging the myths

Despite all the evidence to the contrary, modern economics still implicitly builds on the assumptions associated with the origin myth of money and markets. The idea that money is scarce and a product of the market is central to the neoliberalism which came to dominate economic thinking in the late twentieth and early twenty-first centuries. As mentioned earlier, neoliberalism's handbag economics sees the public sector as a drain upon the market. Public spending should therefore be heavily constrained. There is no place in the neoliberal worldview for a public source of money or an independent public economy.

This ignores the importance historically of non-market state economies in which markets played a minor role. In later chapters I will show how the sovereign power to create and circulate money has been exercised over the centuries, while market dominance of the public money supply in the form of national currency is comparatively recent. What is needed is to reclaim and democratise that sovereign power.

Far from the fairy tale, the alternative story of money presented in this book looks at the evolution of money in relation to social customs and structures of power as well as market forces. Instead of presuming an exclusively economic role for money I will argue that it is necessary to bring into focus the social and public underpinnings of modern money. Particularly public currencies. While all money is a transferable promise there is a vital difference between a pound note and a voucher or a pound and a bitcoin. While a pound is publicly authorised and guaranteed, a voucher depends on the integrity of the issuer and a bitcoin depends on the effectiveness of a computer program. Anything generally accepted as a means of transferring a promise that will be honoured can be seen as money. However, only certain forms of transfer mechanism have the status of publicly authorised money, the public currency.

What is magical about money is its ephemeral nature yet vital social reality. Unlike other economic concepts which have some physical concreteness – land, resources, human labour – money has no 'natural' base. This is particularly true of modern money. As noted earlier, modern fiat money is effectively nothing from nowhere. The dollar, pound or euro represents only a symbol of value and a promise of transferability. As such, money is the most social of things, it is a trust based on a common recognition of the money symbol. The importance of money is revealed by the fact that something identifiable as money occurs in most human societies, even the earliest, which will be explored in the next chapter. The main truth about money that this book will present is that money is a social, political and economic phenomenon. As such, far from the myths of gold and markets, money has many threads to its history. These threads will be taken up in the next three chapters.

TWO

Old magic: money before states and markets

A community without a medium of exchange or a
unit of value has ... never been found.[1]

The fairy tale of the origin of money set out in Box 1.1 saw
money as emerging from the market-like exchange of goods
between individuals through barter. According to the story, the
invention of money created a true market that was able to flexibly
exchange goods. All goods and services could be accessed as
commodities – that is, at a price expressed by money. The value
of each commodity could be represented by the equivalent value
in money. The value of money itself derived from its status as a
commodity. Precious metal was chosen because it was rare and
desired. It was also portable, durable, malleable and divisible.
The use of money was defined by its main market functions as
a yardstick to set and compare prices (unit of account) and as a
means of exchange (which in the last chapter was redefined as
a means of transfer).

The main problem for the fairy story is the lack of historical
evidence. The core assertion that economies were originally
based on moneyless barter cannot be substantiated. Equally,
the link between the origin of money and the development of
markets is not supported by the evidence. Money as coinage,
the form of money associated with the story, is much older than
market-dominated societies. Even if the fairy tale were true,
modern money is fiat and fiduciary (from the Latin *fidere*, to
trust), with no link to precious metal or anything else except

the capacity of the whole economy embraced by the particular money system. This is not to say that money in market economies does not have specific features and functions, but this does not reflect the origin or universality of money itself.

If money is not to be defined by its market form, how is it to be understood? As Alison Hingston Quiggin observes in the quote at the beginning of this chapter, something that can be described as money exists in most, if not all, human communities. It is therefore helpful to an understanding of money to look at its nature and usage before the domination of markets and states. Evidence from pre-market, pre-state societies collected by anthropologists reveals an intriguing range of forms of money. Starting with the stone money of the Yap people of Micronesia (Box 2.1), this chapter will explore some of the best-known examples of traditional monies and see what conclusions can be drawn about their relevance for modern conceptions of money.

Box 2.1: Yap stone money

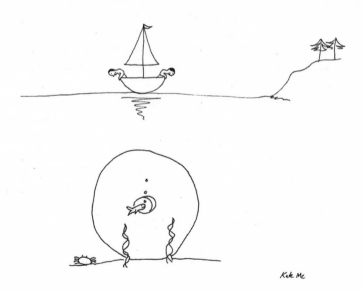

Kik Mc

The Yap people of Micronesia in the South Pacific have a remarkable form of money. It is composed of large circular stones, some of which are up to twelve feet in diameter and weighing thousands of kilos. They would need large numbers of people to transport them.

Each stone is disc shaped, with a hole in the middle so that they can be transported on poles. However, they are not often moved. In fact, one of the most valuable is said to lie at the bottom of the ocean. The Yap money is therefore neither portable nor divisible. It was, however, very valuable, as the stone was quarried on another island and transported by sea – hence the reported loss of one which may have been too heavy for the boat. The limestone of which the stones are made does not occur on Yap, so people travelled hundreds of miles to obtain them, mainly to the island of Palau. In return for the right to quarry the stone, the Yap people traded items such as beads, crops and other goods.

Yap stones were rarely used in trade or for small-scale purchases. Their use was mainly social and political in the context of areas such as marriages, inheritance, symbols of wealth, political deals and alliances or ransom. Nor do people keep the stones as private property; instead they mainly line pathways or sit outside communal buildings. Since, given their size and social importance, the stones do not move, their current ownership is based on social acknowledgement, as are transfers of ownership. The value is not in the size and shape of the stones but their history. Older stones are more highly valued, particularly if they have had notable owners or have been related to some auspicious event.

It is difficult to know exactly how far back the use of stone money goes, or how the Yap people adopted stones as money, but the oral history says the stone was discovered by one of their explorers. It appears to have started with relatively small discs of stone and grown over time. The number created increased after 1871 when a shipwrecked sailor, David O'Keefe, introduced iron tools. However, these later stones were less highly valued and the use of stone money largely ceased after the start of the twentieth century when a more modern currency was adopted.

Shell money

Shell money is arguably the most ubiquitous form of pre-modern money (Boxes 2.2 and 2.3). It was made of shells either as a whole or in parts. Cowrie shells were very common and were small enough to be used whole. They were particularly popular in Africa and traders made vast profits importing them from the Indian Ocean, where they proliferated. Their use was also involved in the slave trade. Like gold and silver, shells were used as both money and ornament. To achieve higher value they were often circulated in strings, famously as wampum in North America. Shell money still persists in very remote communities, but its use largely died out by the end of the nineteenth century.

Shell money is much more like modern ideas of money than the Yap stone. It was used in trade, but also for social and political payments. Shell money was portable and divisible, but it wasn't universal. Different communities valued different shells, in the same way as today's nations have their own currency. However, shell money was often introduced by traders and was not always an indigenous money. The distinctiveness of the shell money could be based on the difficulty in obtaining the shells or the particular way they had been shaped.

Box 2.2: Rossel Island shell money

The people of Rossel Island, Melanesia used shells of different values, with the rarest being the most valuable. The shells came from beaches on the island that were seen as sacred places. They were handed down the generations and very few new ones were added. Different activities were relevant to different shells. Particular shells were required for special events, with less-valued shells being used for small-scale payments. Like the Yap stones, the value of the shell was also enhanced by particular associations and owners.

There were two main types of shell. Dap money was a single shell mainly used by men, and Ko money a string of ten shell discs mainly used by women. The Dap shells were differentiated and categorised, with many of the shells being individually known and named. Payments and transactions often included both Dap and Ko. However, the shells were not interchangeable: payment often required a particular shell. Nor did lower-value shells total up to a higher-value shell, in the way that pence total into pounds. The shells that were most highly regarded were generally in the hands of chiefs, but they could be borrowed, with interest being paid in lower-value shells.

Box 2.3: Wampum

Indigenous North Americans used wampum (from *wampumpeag* meaning 'white strings of shell beads'). White beads represented purity, light, brightness. Darker beads were for more serious things such as war or death. Wampum was made from shells found on the Long Island coast. The beads were produced by coastal tribes and worked into shape mainly by women. Wampum was not used for daily provisioning activities, but was reserved for ceremonial and social purposes such as gift exchange, storytelling, religious ceremonies, recording important treaties and historical events.

The beads were woven into elaborate belts that were evidence of the status and worthiness of the holder. The pattern of the shells was also important. When threaded in a particular way they would transmit a particular message and people were trained in how to 'read' them. This was important for communities with an oral tradition, as wampum belts could be used to record treaties or historical events. Belts would also be exchanged at auspicious ceremonies, such as meetings between tribes or to celebrate a peace treaty.

It was the Europeans who adopted wampum as trading money. A Dutch trader started paying indigenous fur-trappers with wampum strings. Like the Yap stone, wampum started to be mass produced, using metal tools, by both Dutch and other settlers, particularly the British. Manufacturing continued until the early twentieth century. Notably, wampum was declared legal tender in New England in the mid-1600s. Its value was set against copper coin (a white shell was equal to one copper coin; darker shells were more valuable). European settlers tended to ignore the cultural significance of wampum and saw only its commercial value.

Adopting wampum as the means of exchange undermined its social significance as local tribes began to use wampum to trade with each other. Circulating more wampum and using it for trade had other negative consequences. Loss of local wildlife was threatened as fur-trapping of beavers and martens escalated. Trading also saw inter-tribal conflict over whose wampum was to dominate in particular territories.

What can these three examples of traditional money forms tell us about money more widely?

Are stones and shells money?

If money is defined as something originating in market exchange, as the fairy tale would have it, the Yap stones, the Rossel Island shells and North American wampum are not money. They pre-exist both markets and states. Yet they can be adopted effectively as market money, as the experience of cowries and wampum shows. Although they are highly valued, the stones and shells are not an end in themselves, they are a measure of value for other things. For example, for Rossel islanders different social contexts demanded different shells. Wampum belts were constructed with regard to their use, whether for a gift, for a particular leader or a peace treaty.

Like the ideal of precious metal, Yap stones were valuable because they were scarce. However, size and scarcity did not determine value, the social associations of previous ownership and aesthetic appeal were equally, if not more, important. Yap stone, like precious metal, had to be mined, quarried and transported at high cost in labour and other resources. However, Yap stone money was not used for trading as a commercial money. Instead its use was ceremonial and socially prestigious. Similarly, Rossel Island and wampum shells were socially highly prized. This was undermined when the wampum and Yap stones were mass produced for market use.

The ceremonial associations of these traditional monies would seem to give the lie to those who argue that modern money should be based on something rare and valuable. For markets to develop, a much less valuable and plentiful supply of money would seem to be needed. When made more available, shells did become a useful money of transfer, but lost their special significance. They became more like modern money. Cowrie shells became widely used in many countries, so much so that in China some of the early metal money carried the image of cowrie shells.

Having unusual or useful things as money did not cease when societies became states. Early US settlers used tobacco leaves as money. In recent times when economies were in crisis a variety of products became temporary money. For example, as the Soviet Union collapsed in 1991 workers traded a range of exchange items depending on what their factories made. This was not barter exchange, which implies that each participant gets what they want. People accepted jars of pickled cabbage as payment not because they wanted pickled cabbage, but because they hoped to transfer the pickled cabbage in a later trade. As such, pickled cabbage became the means of transfer of value. When the jar of pickled cabbage was put on the larder shelf to be consumed, it ceased to be money.

Yap stones and shells did, however, share one feature with precious-metal money: they had little use value except as ornaments or cultural symbols. Other forms of traditional money were both useful and not inherently scarce. An example is cloth money.

Useful magic: cloth money

In the early 1950s the anthropologist Mary Douglas recorded the use of raffia cloths among the Lele people in what is now the Democratic Republic of Congo. The cloths were woven by men and boys and took quite a lot of preparation to make. They were worn by both men and women, and as they wore out in a few months, a replacement was constantly necessary. Two cloths sewn together made one skirt. Up to ten lengths made a ceremonial man's skirt and the most highly valued were richly embroidered.

A major use of the cloths was the payment of marriage dues, but gifts of raffia cloths were involved in all social relations. They circulated among family members, in celebration of special occasions, parting gifts, to celebrate a birth or mourn a death. They were presented as tribute to chiefs. Exchanged reciprocally in more formal contexts, they indicated status and avoided giving offence. Gifting and exchanging of cloths linked young and old, and different clans or villages. Entrance fees in cloths were paid to gain membership of cults or age-set groups. Cloths were also used to pay blood-compensation in case of injury, or other fines for misbehaviour. However, distressingly from the perspective of today, buying and selling women was the main use of the raffia skirts. The value of a woman in 1950 was equivalent to that of a slave – one hundred cloths.

The number of cloths required for different occasions was fixed by custom. Twenty cloths should be given to a father by a son on achieving adulthood; twenty cloths should be given to a wife on the birth of a child; marriage dues were fifty to the father and forty to the mother; entrance to a cult group was a hundred cloths, as was a fee to those who could divine fates or officiate at healing rites. Social misdemeanours such as fighting ranged from two cloths upwards, while adultery damages were a hundred cloths.

While the cloths were exchanged between individuals, such as sons to fathers, the main focus, marriage and the transfer of women, could involve the whole community. Each village chose a trustworthy and eloquent person to be spokesperson and treasurer. Villages could end up in debt to each other over insults, injuries or failure to pay sufficient bride dues. Such debts would be paid by a levy on each of the village clans. Nevertheless, there was extensive use of borrowing to pay for high-value events such as marriages. The borrowers did not repay the loan of the cloth, but were expected to reciprocate in due course by lending in the future. Although men and boys could always clear any raffia debts by creating more cloths, they tended to borrow rather than weave new cloths. Nor were the cloths stockpiled; they were borrowed or otherwise used.

The Lele had a complex approach to trading in, or with, the cloths. Within related groups, goods were transferred with a notional payment of a small number of cloths. Outside of these kinship networks raffia cloths were traded with other tribal groups for a range of products. As a result, the Lele cloths were widely circulated in the region. In some of the external communities they were used for clothing; in others where people did not wear raffia clothes, the cloths were used purely as money for future trade or payment.

Douglas noted that other forms of money were creeping in, most notably Belgian franc coins. The franc coins were much less highly valued than the raffia. Douglas records that she could not buy ordinary objects that she needed, even though she offered double the amount of francs to the usual rate of francs to cloths. Nor could she easily get hold of any cloths, as no one would sell her one for francs. However, the Lele did need Belgian francs to pay taxes and fines. As the raffia was considered too valuable to sell for francs, the young would lend francs to the elderly to make their payments.

The cloth money introduces another dimension. Shells and stones as money don't generally have another purpose. However, the raffia cloth is worn as clothing. Like other useful things that have been adopted as money – cattle, grain, knives, hatchets or blankets – the question is, when is a blanket a blanket and when is it money? The answer to the latter question, must be when the blanket is used as a guide to value or is accepted with the intention of future transfer. The Lele raffia cloths also differ from the shells and stone money in that they are not inherently scarce. Yap stones had to be brought hundreds of miles. Shells often came from distant coasts. Lele cloths were manufactured by Lele men and boys. The creation of their money was in their own hands. This did not seem to cause problems. Cloths did not 'flood the market', as is the fear with modern fiat money, yet no one limited production.

Like the use of wampum and cowrie shells, the cloths were used in areas of trade, but they did not originate in trade. Traditional ceremonial and other social activities appear to be the original, and often dominant, use. This would indicate that the social origin of money was prior to its adoption for market exchange. Failure to recognise the importance of ceremonial money, and an aversion to trade on the part of many traditional communities, led to major miscalculations by Western explorers.

Box 2.4: The wrong magic

Henry Morton Stanley (1841–1904) made several journeys to explore Africa in the 1870s. Most famously, he found the missionary David Livingstone and travelled to the source of the Nile. For his journey through the Congo in 1874–77 he took a large amount of traditional money forms – cloth, copper wire and beads – to enable him to trade for food and canoes. To carry this together with his other equipment he recruited more than two hundred local people. However, rather than bartering his way across Africa, he was often in conflict with local communities who refused to trade. More than a half of his total party of over three hundred died through disease, hunger, drowning and killing, or they deserted.

Quiggin argues that Westerners such as Stanley misunderstood the symbolism of traditional forms of money such as brass rods or beads. They tended to see them as neutral objects that could be used in trade, rather than as symbolic forms of money relating to relationships, customs and rituals. They failed to see that it was not the object itself that was seen as valuable. One brass rod or cloth was not the same as any other brass rod or cloth. Like today's currencies, they were not interchangeable. Banknotes may take the same form, pieces of decorated paper, but it is no use trying to pay with a pound note in France. Similarly cloths, wire and beads may superficially look the same, but they did not have the same cultural resonance in different societies.

Quiggin rejects trade as the main factor in the evolution of money. What she called 'simple societies' did not need a money standard for their basic provisioning as this was carried out in kinship networks. The origin of money lay in social relationships. Where money was needed – both as a yardstick of value and as a means of transfer – was to meet marriage payments and what she describes as blood revenge (wergild). This refers to the extensive use of money payments in the case of injury or death. It was these two areas that required established standards of value and a regularised medium of transfer. Quiggin concluded that 'when once a system of conventional gifts or payments with a definite scale of values has been established (and this is necessary for bride-price and for wergild) the first steps are taken in the evolution of money'.[2]

With the rejection of the myth of the origin of money in the need to overcome the limitations of barter in the exchange of commodities as claimed in the fairy tale in Box 1.1, the question became what, in traditional societies, was the link with modern, market–oriented forms of money? Leading anthropologists came up with a new dynamic, reciprocity.

Communal magic: reciprocity

> Our conception of money and the practice of buying and selling for the purpose of acquiring it for personal enrichment are seldom met with among simpler societies.[3]

As an early student of traditional money, Quiggin took issue with the economic assumptions about the role of barter. She rejects the barter theory about money overcoming the problem of matching exchanges, by pointing out that there were no such inconveniences in traditional societies. There is no direct exchange or barter because interactions extend over time, involving a range of customs and expectations. She also argues that Westerners had a fundamental misunderstanding about the traditional forms and use of money.

Anthropologists differed about how to understand the elaborate rituals that accompanied forms of economic exchange. In 1922 Bronislaw Malinowski, an anthropologist at the London School of Economics, published his famous study of the Trobriand Islander's Kula ring in his book, *Argonauts of the Western Pacific*. The Kula ring was an elaborate ritual between island communities that involved long sea voyages to ceremonially circulate highly prized armbands and necklaces around the islands. Malinowski saw the Kula ring as an exercise designed to maintain good relationships between powerful individuals across the archipelago. The Kula travelled around in a full circle, the armbands going one way, the necklaces in the opposite direction.

Alongside the Kula ceremonies, goods of various sorts were exchanged mainly through a process of mutual gift-giving with previous contacts. Malinowski did not think the Kula objects could be seen as early money because they were so imbued with magical, spiritual and cultural significance. Also, they could not be identified as having a specific value. Nevertheless there was a provisioning logic to the perilous journeys. The islands in the archipelago varied in geography and resources. Some were large and lush, others more barren, requiring the importation of food. On the more barren islands other skills developed, such as pottery-making and canoe-building. While the main focus was the ceremonial transfer of the armbands and necklaces, long-term reciprocal relationships were built up across the islands with the obligation on all parties to provide goods to trade, and to offer hospitality and assistance where necessary.

On the individual islands Malinowski found that there was extensive communal labour in the building of canoes or work in the gardens that provided their food. This form of labour was based on custom rather than power, although the higher-status gardens would be done first. There was social prestige in being involved in this communal work. The motivation was participation, not payment.

The French anthropologist Marcel Mauss argued that there was much more linkage between traditional forms of money and the modern version. What mattered was whether the symbolic items that were exchanged fulfilled some of the functions of money. Did they have recognised comparative value and was the transfer of the object seen as a payment of an obligation or debt? He argued that they did. There were recognisable scales of value of objects against each other.

While Malinowski thought that the items ritually exchanged were so charged with magical and cultural symbols that they could not be seen as money, Mauss did not think the magical nature was a barrier to them fulfilling recognisably monetary functions. The expectations embedded in the exchange were formalised and the items could be seen as making payments. These arrangements could be between different groups, such as 'silent trade' where communities leave gifts for each other. A fishing community would leave fish, while forest dwellers might leave fruits.

Mauss's approach differed from both Malinowski's rejection of the various talismans as money things and the claims of economists such as Menger that money emerged out of barter. In his 1925 essay, *The Gift*, Mauss made the case for recognising reciprocity as a major stage in the evolution of human societies, and thereby important in understanding the origin of money. In opposition to the Western obsession with economic exchange based on economic utility and individual benefit through barter and haggling, Mauss argued that exchange in traditional societies was based on reciprocity.

This meant that most exchange was not carried out in a market-like manner, it was more socially conducted through networks of giving and receiving, with broad reciprocity being achieved over time. This made early provisioning more like mutual aid or welfare systems rather than market exchange. Reciprocal provisioning had a moral foundation of obligation and entitlement rather than a calculation of maximising individual economic benefit. Generosity was encouraged, rather than parsimony. Reciprocity was aimed at building communities and relationships, rather than accumulating assets. It prioritised the well-being of communities, rather than personal riches.

Mauss's approach resonated with later anthropologists. Marshall Sahlins in his 1972 book, *Stone Age Economics*, identified three types of exchange; Gift or Generalised Reciprocity, where there is not expected to be exact equivalence and the balance of the relationship evolves over time; Balanced or Symmetrical Reciprocity, which entails an equivalence between participants; and Market or Negative Reciprocity, where each party tries to maximise their own advantage.

From the work of Mauss it would seem that, historically, there is a much stronger case for reciprocity as the origin of money than for barter. Money's roots are in society, not the market. However, reciprocity still assumes two equal participants in the exchange – that is, it keeps some of the elements of the barter theory. Barter and reciprocity are both based on the notion of exchange. Barter is envisaged as a market-like interaction at the individual level; reciprocity is also assumed to be an interaction between individuals or a group. The exchange may be over time, but there is a strong element of equivalence.

The theory of money's origin in reciprocity is a great improvement on the theory of barter. It has the benefit of anthropological evidence, but it still has some limitations. The focus is still upon a commodity-like exchange of goods and services, albeit informally and over time. What this misses is the wider use of money in pre-state and pre-market societies. This is why it is helpful to move away from the assumption of exchange and equivalence as the primary focus of money, in favour of the broader concept of transfer. A transfer may go in only one direction, as a tribute or tax payment, a contribution or donation or, as will be discussed later, an issue of new money. To widen the focus we need to look at all the ways in which money-like calculations are made in traditional society. To do that we can borrow an alliteration from another fairy story.

Fe Fe Fi Fi Fo Fo: the use of money in pre-modern societies

In the fairy tale *Jack and the Beanstalk*, magic beans grow into a huge beanstalk. Climbing to the top, Jack is confronted by a giant who thunders 'Fe Fi Fo Fum' to terrifying effect. Modern economies can be seen as giants at the end of a historical beanstalk. They would seem to have little in common with small, pre-market, pre-state societies, but there is more to connect them than would first appear. This linkage can be captured as 'Fe Fe Fi Fi Fo Fo' which stands for feast, fees, fines, fidelity, force, formality. I want to argue that broadening the focus in this way will be more illuminating for understanding modern money than the preoccupation with markets or patterns of reciprocity.

Superficially it would seem that there is a great difference between the use of money in traditional societies and modern commodified market systems. Customary forms of money appear to be rarely used for trading within societies, and not often for trading between societies. Internal provisioning is generally based on family or group cooperation and reciprocity. External trade is sometimes by direct barter, but more often carried out through long-standing complex interactions disguised as gift exchange.

In non-market societies money has a predominantly non-commercial use. There are not general-purpose money things such as dollars or euros. Different items can be used for specific purposes. High-value forms of money may be reserved for special forms of payment such as for a marriage or making amends for a serious misdemeanour. As discussed earlier, money is about the transfer of value, but what is valued and the measure, mechanism and context of that value can be very different. The money object may have traditional, emotional or sacred connotations.

I want to argue that looking at money through a market lens misses some key connections between the two ends of the beanstalk. There are other uses of money in modern 'giant' societies that have clear origins in the roots of traditional preoccupations.

Feast

In many traditional communities money objects play a major part in communal activities. A well-known example is the potlatch, a gift-giving feast, widely practised by indigenous people on the north-west coast of North America. Potlatches took place on ceremonial occasions, when community leaders vied with each other to see who could give away or burn the most valued objects such as animal skins, blankets and copper ornaments. The authorities in the region banned such activities, which they saw as destructive and against the principle of the accumulation of wealth.

Feasts and festivals may also have accompanied communal activity. It is thought that Stonehenge in the UK was built over three thousand years ago by willing hands with considerable amounts of festivity. This conclusion was drawn by finding huge amounts of animal bones nearby, many of which had been brought hundreds of miles. There are many modern examples of feasts and festivals with the use of bonfires and fireworks, although rarely the communal burning of valued objects. However, there is an expectation that rich people will demonstrate their superior status by the disbursement of their wealth in charitable activities and foundations.

Fees

A traditional use of money, whether as a measure of value or also as the means of transfer, is the payment of fees. For men in particular, there were often societies or age-related structures which they needed to join if they were to participate in joint activities such as hunting or social events. Fees were also payable to people with special skills such as predicting the future, carrying out healing rituals or other intercessions with spiritual forces.

Fees are an important aspect of modern society. Membership of political parties, religious organisations, hobby clubs or sports organisations often requires a fee to be paid. Sometimes this is for a particular service such as the right to use a golf course, but often the membership in itself is the important thing. Governments and other public bodies also charge fees, such as for the right to drive a car or to get a new passport or other public documentation. Fees are also charged by the private sector for professional services. As with most of the activities related to money in this book, the payment of fees takes place across social, public and commercial contexts.

Fines

The imposition of fines is widely reported in the anthropological literature. In societies with no rule of law or enforcement agencies, conflict can be very dangerous. One of the central functions of money is to provide a yardstick against which the relative seriousness of the transgression is judged. The payment need not be in the money thing, but whatever form it takes needs to be seen as equivalent to the money value expressed. Injury payments were very important in traditional societies as a compensation for damage.

Today, fines are more likely to be imposed for injuries sustained at work or through medical negligence or other accident for which some person or organisation was at fault. Fining is not generally used today for more serious crimes, as these are dealt with by incarceration. Fines are mainly limited to less serious offences, although they can be high for activities such as fraud.

Fidelity

This addresses payments as a symbol of loyalty, as a tribute to a leader or revered person. Tribute is an ambiguous word. It has positive and negative connotations. Most dictionaries define tribute as an act, statement or gift that is intended to show gratitude, respect or admiration. At the same time it is often used interchangeably with a tax. In Latin the word *tributum* means a thing contributed or paid, while the word *tribuere* translates as to pay, assign or grant. Perhaps the most important word here is contribution. A tribute imposed by force would not imply fidelity.

As well as tribute to communal leaders, payments may be made to cultural or religious leaders. Even small communities often have a shrine, temple or sacred place. Money can be used to pay for priests, building religious centres, propitiating the gods. Most current religions retain the concept of giving money or labour to enable the religion to prosper and grow. These are often funded by tithes, the giving of a fixed amount of income or wealth.

Force

While in traditional societies tribute may be paid by consent, it is important to recognise that it can also be imposed by force. More belligerent communities may engage in capture and ransom, or extract payments from other communities under threat of violence. Equally, local chiefs may demand tribute through coercion.

Transfer of money and other items of value under threat of force continues to this day. Colonialism and imperial conquest saw traditional communities forced into waged work, or the sale of their products, to earn the money to pay for the imposition of taxes in the conqueror's currency. States still have the power to enforce taxation. Social and commercial demands for payment can also be imposed by law. Not least, there are criminal ways of extorting money.

Formality

This is arguably the most important use of money in traditional societies. Most social events such as births, deaths, marriages, coming of age are accompanied by the use of the money object to mark the solemnity or celebration of the occasion. The form, method and level of payments are often prescribed. Particularly important are the payments made in the negotiation of marriage. This has been interpreted in various ways. At worst it can be seen as trading women as a commodity. At best, a large payment is evidence of the capacity of the groom or his family to provide well for the bride in the future. The money object is also used for important social events, as in the wearing of ornate wampum belts or highly embroidered raffia skirts. The money object may also be used formally as gifts in external interaction with other, possibly, hostile groups.

The expectation of the use of money at key events is still very important. Weddings can involve high levels of expenditure. Prestige events require pomp and splendour. Baby showers are becoming increasingly popular, with the expectations of gifts in advance of the birth. Retirements, wedding anniversaries, funerals all assume relevant amounts of expenditure.

Magic money: ancient and modern

My argument in this chapter is that once we have dispensed with the myths of money as being linked to precious metal and the market, we can see connecting threads between ancient and modern money. These threads are in the social and political use of money. Money is used mainly to mark important social events and avoid internal and external sources of conflict.

However, there is some overlap with the fairy story in that traditional forms of money do have intrinsic value. Like the mythical origin of money in the intrinsic value of gold and silver, pre-modern forms of money are highly valued in themselves. Sometimes this is based on rarity, other times on human effort such as shaping shells or weaving cloth. The value of a traditional money may lie in the history of the money thing itself, such as having a prestigious previous owner. But what the various forms of traditional money do not have is a market value. They are most definitely not commodities. They may also not be transferable. Yap stones may not physically change hands, wampum belts may be worn only by people of a certain status.

What they all do have is a major monetary function, the ability to enable the value of people, things, cultural or political events, to be compared. The more elaborate the wampum belt, the higher the status of the wearer, or the importance of the occasion in which it is presented to another person or group. The more serious the injury, the more the guilty person must pay. None of these equates to a price on the market.

I would argue that the case for having an intrinsically valuable form of money is much stronger in a cultural, social or political context than the market. The weakness of the myth of money's origin in precious-metal money, which is at the heart of the fairy tale in Box 1.1, is that it is inherently limited. The problem is that the scarcity associated with precious metal is not compatible with the need of markets for a large-scale, readily available, transfer medium. Unlike speculative and expanding market economies, traditional societies did not need large amounts of transfer money. Money was not central to provisioning the community, as this was achieved mainly by subsistence cultivation and reciprocity. The main need for money was as a yardstick for identifying comparative values and a money object that can fulfil a symbolic role.

The continuity of the social nature and use of money in non-market, non-state communities with money today lies in its cultural, social and political aspects. Money is not bound to the market-place. It is not just a neutral way of measuring price on the market. It is a symbol of monetary identity and social and public trust. Even more so now that it has dispensed with any claim to inherent value. The threads of the ancient social use of money are still with us, as is the political evolution of money, which will be explored in the next chapter.

THREE

The king was in his counting house: money and the state

'The king was in his counting house, counting out his money' is a line from a traditional nursery rhyme 'Sing a Song of Sixpence'. For king read sovereign. The sovereign is the one who rules, who may be a king, queen, tyrant, priest, president, parliament or sovereign people. Sovereign money is money created or controlled by whoever or whatever the ruler or ruling structure may be. This is a very different perspective on money from the forms of money in the last chapter whose origin is lost in tradition, or the spontaneous emergence of money in the market as the fairy tale in Box 1.1 would have it. Sovereign money is based on the concrete exercise of power.

The sovereign power to create money

Kate Mc

Sovereign money overlaps with, but is not the same as, the public currency, particularly in the modern era. Sovereign money is the public currency created and circulated by the sovereign power. Today that power often rests with central banks, which, as the next chapter will illustrate, hold an ambivalent position between the sovereign state and the banking sector. In many states, the power to create the public currency is also subsumed by the banking sector itself. In contrast, this chapter discusses the historical and continuing role of ruling authorities in the administration of money.

Sovereign money differs from the traditional money discussed in the last chapter. Traditional money has the authority of custom. Those with higher status may exercise rights in relation to the traditional form of money, but they are not seen as the source of that money, nor can they determine its form or value. As we have seen, money in non-market societies was mainly related to social contexts: marriages, disputes, tributes. Most provisioning was done on a subsistence basis. This does not mean that economic transfers did not take place at all, but they were peripheral to the organisation of the society.

Sovereign money also differs from the fairy-story origin of money in trade. It emerged much earlier in human civilisation and was not dominated by precious metal. Forms of state money and accounting existed long before precious-metal coin and widespread markets. Unlike the fairy tale's benign view of money emerging from industrious bartering communities, money's sovereign history is associated with power, conflict and national identity. Rather than lubricating a self-organising market, money is strongly connected with other forms of sovereign power, most notably taxation. Nor is money seen as a naturally occurring phenomenon. It has to be organised and maintained, a task which is the responsibility of sovereigns, most recently exhibited in the state rescue of the banking sector following the 2007–08 financial crash.

In discussing the political history of money it is important to separate the history of money from the history of precious-metal coinage. While coinage was central to the development of sovereign money systems in Europe, as well as being key to the myths and assumptions of the fairy story, it is only one of the forms sovereign money can take. The central role of the state in relation to money long precedes the invention of precious-metal coinage.

Money through the ages

Sumer was one of the first civilisations to emerge, around 5000 BCE, in the region that is now Iraq. It was located on highly productive agricultural land in the fertile plain between the two great rivers, Tigris and Euphrates. Large-scale agricultural production and irrigation was led by religious leaders with temples as centres of administration. Sumer had a centralised distribution system. Symbols were used to keep track of what came in to the centre and what went out. Early pictograms appeared to be direct representations of products such as grain, sheep, goats, cattle and pigs. It is thought that these representations led to the development of writing around 3500 BCE. An early development of money is thought to relate to barley as a staple crop. Barley was stored in warehouses and gross weights of barley were represented by silver coins called shekels. The size of the coins themselves was also standardised on their weight in barley, usually 180 grains.

China provides an example of the range of forms of money that a state can adopt. Burial evidence indicates that cowrie shells were in use around 1000 BCE and remained so well into the Common Era, possibly as late as 1300 CE. By 500 BCE metals were being used, such as copper, lead, tin, iron, bronze and brass. These were made into a variety of shapes, including representations of cowries, knives or spades. China, at the time, was made up of many separate societies and states in which control of money was a major feature. Goetzman records that when the Tian family took power in the city of Linzi around 386 BCE, they made knife shapes with a motto that translates as 'construct the nation'. He also draws attention to a document of the same era that argues that money is a much more useful instrument of power than force through imperial decree.[1]

The Qin dynasty in the third century BCE united China and created what became the world's most long-lasting coin. It was a bronze disc with a square hole in the centre that enabled it to be threaded onto strings. These were known as cash, hence the name commonly used for coinage. Strings of cash were used for centuries, at least until the end of the nineteenth century.

As sovereign-controlled money, Chinese metal money was mainly used for public salaries and paying taxes and fines. Like most states, Chinese coin-minting was official. However, private mints continually popped up which were sometimes tolerated and at other times shut down. China also made the first use of paper money. In the period 806–21 CE, when facing a severe shortage of copper, the most prized form of money, the emperor authorised the issue of paper money.

The Song dynasty (960–1279) also considered copper to be too valuable to be used as money and an alternative iron currency was too unwieldy. Needing a usable supply of money for state purposes, including maintaining soldiers to secure the borders, it created paper money. This was printed on mulberry-bark paper, which made it strong enough to be passed from hand to hand. The link to cash was maintained by the images of strings of coins on the paper notes. At first, private bankers were given authority to issue the paper money, but the system crashed and printing of paper notes was monopolised by the state in 1160. This era also saw the state take on entrepreneurial activities such as trading in tea and making loans.

Kublai Khan (1215–94) went further and decreed that paper money should be the main circulating medium. An imperial mint was set up in the late 1200s. The explorer Marco Polo, who lived in China from 1271 to 1292, is recorded as being amazed at a government-issued paper money not backed by precious metal. China is therefore notable for developing the first sovereign paper money that exists by fiat – that is, by state authority alone.

In China, Marco Polo found a money system where the state paid for all its needs in paper money. This money was then readily circulated among traders. Merchants visiting the country were relieved of their valuables and given paper money in its place, which they could later use to re-buy their valuables. Local traders were also encouraged to swap valuables (metal, jewellery and so on) for generous paper payment. Traders were then entitled to buy any goods they chose with the paper money. According to

Polo's account, there was no fixed limit to the amount of money issued and circulated.

It is notable that in the early history of money in China gold and silver plays no part and the use of paper money breaks the link with metal completely. This was not the case in Europe, where the lure of gold had a stranglehold on the monetary system. Far from the flexibility of the Chinese approach, the fairy story and the ideal of precious-metal money held sway.

The Midas touch

The legend of King Midas, which may or may not be based on a real ruler, is about the lure of gold. According to Greek myth, Midas was granted the magical power to turn everything he touched into gold. As a result, he starved to death as all his food turned into gold. As we shall see, there are dangers in the lust for gold.

Precious metal, mainly silver, was widely used in the ancient world, but the idea of moulding soft metals into coins emerged around 600–700 BCE. The Persians, Indians and Greeks were the first to make extensive use of coins made of electrum, a naturally occurring amalgam of gold and silver. The invention of coinage is often associated with the ancient kingdom of Lydia (now in Turkey), where the coins were first used by both traders and rulers. One of the earliest hoard of coins was found during the excavation of a temple, which would indicate some religious use. It is very unlikely that the coins were used for everyday trading, as they were too valuable. This is a recurrent feature of precious-metal money. It was so valuable that it was mainly used in very high-status activities, far from the mundane trading envisaged in the fairy tale.

The early precious-metal coins that did circulate widely were small and irregular in shape and as they were made of pure metal they were weighed to establish their value. At first there was little indication of where the coins were minted and any markings were often images of animals. As coinage spread through the Greek civilisation, names appeared on the coins and key images were associated with particular city-states. As substantial numbers of the coins have not been found in far-flung locations this would indicate that they were not widely used in long-distance trade. Also their main local use was not trade; rather, they were used in the pursuit of war through empire-building and the constant conflicts in the Mediterranean region.

The historical evidence would lead to the conclusion that if precious-metal coinage had any monetary origin it was in war, not the market. Conflicts were largely dependent on mercenaries, who fought for whoever would pay them. Silver was the main metal of payment. It was used in imperial wars and when rich lineages fought each other for the prize of being overall ruler.

Central to the political history of money is sovereign identity and power.

Coinage as talisman: conflict and power

The ability to establish a distinctive currency is a major demonstration of sovereign power. This is the case from ancient China, through the emergence of coinage in Greece, to the twentieth century where large numbers of new nations emerged from colonialism with a new national money as a major symbol of nationhood together with the flag and the anthem. This makes political experiments such as the euro an interesting test of the nature of money. Can a currency exist without a political frame? This question will be addressed in Chapter Six.

One of the earliest uses of coin-minting to support empire-building was the rise of the Macedonians. King Philip II of Macedonia (359 BCE–336 BCE) used his control of gold mines to fund what was a huge army for that era. It was partly a standing army and partly mercenary. More famously, his son Alexander, who became ruler of Macedonia in 336 BCE following the murder of his father, made great military use of coin. He was twenty years old when he came to power, and waged war almost continually until he died in 323 BCE, aged thirty-three, of natural causes.

During his long military career Alexander led an invasion of Persia (present-day Iran) and defeated every army across North Africa to Egypt and to India. Alexander used up to half a ton of silver a day to pay his soldiers and, where necessary, appease enemies. He had more than twenty mints producing coins, which had images of gods and heroes and the word *Alexandrou* (of Alexander). This money was trusted because of the metal content, and also the authenticity of its minting. As well as paying mercenaries, the coinage was used for other state purposes, including the payment of taxes.

The third century BCE saw Rome adopt coinage. The word 'mint' stems from that time. However, coins were not widely used, as this was in the period of the Republic (500 BCE– 27 BCE) and the era of the great philosophers. Aristotle is recorded as deriding the desire for money and Plato argued that the Philosopher Kings should not engage with such worldly objects. As the republic began to break down and the imperial era approached, the minting of coin was widespread and associated with the search for power. Julius Caesar consolidated control of the currency in his hands and his own image. The first emperor, Augustus (63 BCE–14 CE), made full use of that control and new emperors would signal their arrival by issuing a new coinage.

Roman coins were made from a variety of metals: bronze, brass, copper, gold and silver. The silver denarius became one of the most widely used coins. The Romans also had to face a modern problem, the need for more coinage than precious metal would allow. Much of this money was needed to fund imperial wars. This led to debasement, dilution of the precious-metal content and the use of base metal. The Roman empire spread the use of coinage widely, but when the empire failed the use of coinage diminished, and even ceased completely in Britain.

The widespread use of precious-metal currency was re-established by the innovations of the Holy Roman Emperor Charlemagne, Charles the Great (742–814), who ruled most of Western and Central Europe. He set up a currency system based on 240 pennies minted from a pound of silver. Charlemagne demanded that the coins be pure silver so that they would be interchangeable. The pennies became established as the denier in France, the pfennig in Germany, the dinero in Spain, the denari in Italy and the penny in Britain. The structure of pounds, shillings and pence was maintained in Britain until the currency was decimalised in 1971 in anticipation of joining the European Economic Community (later the European Union).

However, in earlier periods the main use of precious metal was not trade but the politics of war and conflict. After losing the Battle of Maldon against the Danes in 991, King Æthelred (the Unready, 966–1016) paid a large ransom to the Danish king. This 'danegeld' was paid in the hope of avoiding further bloodshed. The most famous ransom in English history is that paid to secure the freedom of King Richard I (Box 3.1).

Box 3.1: A king's ransom

A 'king's ransom' is a way of describing a very large amount of money. This is not just an idle phrase. Precious-metal money was extensively used for ransom payment during conflict. War was a major part of elite life, and the capture of a high-status prisoner was a great prize. In 1192 Richard I (Richard the Lionheart, 1157–99) was returning from fighting in one of the many crusades that tried to dislodge the Muslim occupiers from Jerusalem. He had the misfortune to be shipwrecked in the Mediterranean and had to take the dangerous course of crossing Europe by land. He was captured by the Duke of Austria, who handed him over to the Holy Roman Emperor, Henry VI, who demanded the equivalent of 100,000 pounds of silver. This was two to three times the English kingdom's income. Richard's mother, Eleanor of Aquitaine, raised the money by taxing both clergy and laymen's property and confiscating the gold and silver treasures of the church.

The Middle Ages also saw the Hundred Years' War (1337–1453) between the kings of England and France, famous for the sacrifice of Joan of Arc in the battle for Orleans. In 1356 King John II of France was captured by the Black Prince (Edward III). John was eventually freed in 1360, ceding a third of western France and paying the huge sum of three million crowns. Even then, it was only a partial release, as other hostages took his place, including his son. The ransom was so large that payments continued to be made until the reign of Henry V (1413–22).

The insatiable European lust for gold and silver drove violence and cruelty in the New World. When explorers realised that the Incas, who lived in what is now Peru, had huge deposits of gold and silver they subjugated the people and sailed back with their loot. The Incas did not see gold and silver as money; instead, it was used for religious and ornamental purposes. What the Incas valued more than metal was the land and natural resources. Food production was based on control of the land, which was divided equally between the emperor, the priests and the people. Production was planned, people paid taxes through their labour and received an allocation of food. When the Spanish came they captured the gold and put the indigenous people to work in the mines.

Money and militarism were closely linked in European history. The era of mercantilism that dominated Europe until the emergence of industrialism was based on military support of trade with foreign colonies and the calculation of a nation's wealth by its ownership of precious metal, or bullion. European countries fought with each other to safeguard trading posts and trade routes. Spanish treasure ships from the New World were closely guarded by warships. Any less well protected merchant ships were harassed by official and unofficial pirates. A problem arose when areas of the world with desirable goods, such as China, refused to trade in return. In the early nineteenth century British silver piled up in China through its exports of silk, porcelain and tea. Britain retaliated by launching the Opium Wars to force China to import Indian opium and pay for it in silver.

While mercantilism was a struggle over the control of precious metal, control of other forms of money is equally important in conflicts.

Money and national identity

One of the drivers in the American War of Independence was the refusal of the British to allow the settlers to create their own currency. Differing forms of money were also evident in the American Civil War. The South funded itself by issuing bonds based on the cotton trade. Bonds are promises to pay a specific sum in a particular currency at a future date. The South's plan was thwarted when the North blockaded Southern ports and the cotton bonds could not be redeemed. The North funded itself in a very modern way by issuing thousands of 'greenbacks' – the forerunner of the modern dollar. This was secured on nothing but people's trust in the broad economic capacity of the North. The modern dollar is backed by the same economic trust.

In times of war or when states start to break down the ownership and control of money becomes very important. A modern example is the battle of the banknotes in Libya. Following the Western-led overthrow of President Gaddafi in 2011, the ensuing civil war split Libya broadly into two opposing would-be governments vying for supremacy. One was centred on Tripoli, the other on Tobruk. Building on the previously existing banking infrastructure, each putative government claimed to own the central bank. The strength of the central bank in Tobruk was the rumour that it had $185 million in gold and silver coins, but the central bank in Tripoli was thought to have the codes to open the vault. By 2016 it looked as if each putative government would have its own central bank, printing its own version of the national currency, the dinar. There was another divide as well. The Tripoli central bank used the Western note-printers De La Rue, the Eastern Tobruk central bank used Russian-made banknotes.

However, the country as a whole faced a severe shortage of money. In the uncertainty of conflict people were holding on to their money as cash (notes and coin), rather than circulate it through the banking system as electronic transfers. The amount of money held in bank accounts fell by 50% between 2013 and 2015. By 2017, 70% of money was held in cash, compared with 9% in 2010. This created a huge demand for banknotes. In the end the need for cash currency was so great that both sets of notes were widely circulated. The main differences were the serial numbers and the signatures of the governors of the central bank.

Today, even where there is not civil war, national currencies are still a potential area of conflict. Where once nations fought each other to accumulate gold, countries are vying with each other to get the best trading advantage from the relative value of their currencies. States also hold reserves of each other's currencies, particularly the dollar. More than 60% of reserves across the globe are held in dollars, a good proportion by China. At one level, countries using and holding each other's currencies could be seen as a good thing, fulfilling the promise of neoliberalism by turning the world into one large economy. On the other hand, holding a nation's currency reflects a potential call on its labour and resources. Given that globalised trading and finance have produced almost unlimited amounts of money designated in national currencies, it is the people in those nations who will have to honour that money.

In the modern world there is a strong link between national currencies and nation-states. This is not total. The euro is a supranational currency, and some countries either officially or unofficially use another country's currency, usually the dollar. Within national economies we take it for granted that there will be enough money in circulation to meet our needs and that its face-value will be honoured. A ten-dollar bill will always be worth ten dollars. But this was not always the case. The existence and value of national currencies had to be established and maintained. This was a role for the state, not the market.

In Europe this was complicated by the lust for gold, particularly in Britain. While precious metal was not the original form of money that the fairy tale claims, the assumption that this was the case played a notable role in the development of the British national currency and the approach to currencies in general. Far from gold and silver being the real, natural form of money, the adoption of precious-metal coinage was more of a hindrance than a help in developing a public currency suitable for expanding market economies.

Maintaining the illusion

According to the fairy tale in Box 1.1, the original form of money was something valued in itself. Gold, silver and other prized metals seem to have had a magical allure, a Midas touch that attracts people to them. As a result, everything else is seen as a poor substitute. This has led to a perspective on money that has strongly influenced monetary policy, particularly in Europe. As noted earlier, like gold and silver, modern money is seen as being in short supply, despite the fact that it no longer has even a remote connection with precious metal and is made of base metal, paper and electronic dots.

The source of this confused approach to modern money reflects the fact that precious-metal money was extensively used in Europe and formed the basis of its early coinage. The benefit of precious metal acting as a measure is that it has a standard weight. The earliest forms of precious-metal money were metal lumps rather than coins. These were weighed to verify their purity. When the metals were made into coin there was less emphasis on weighing and more on counting. The measure of value was the number of coins. This led to an uneasy relationship between counting and weighing coins. Did it matter if the coins were impure, as long as they enabled measurement and transfer to be achieved? European rulers struggled to maintain a balance between the desire for purity and the need for sufficient coin.

When the Holy Roman Emperor Charlemagne (742–814) set up his new currency system he based it on coins minted from a pound of silver. His aim in using pure metal was to create money that could be trusted across his empire. However, within a couple of hundred years the coins were widely debased. The punishment for debasing coinage by private minters could be severe. Many were hanged or had their hands cut off. However, rulers were also guilty themselves of debasing coins. Purity was difficult to maintain as coin-minting was widespread, and people of rank from dukes to bishops claimed the authority to mint. Harvard lawyer Christine Desan has described the difficulties the British state had in maintaining a viable and sufficient coinage from as early as the eleventh century.[2]

The problem was a choice between having a lower number of purer coins or a larger circulation of debased coins. The face-value of the coins was also set by the sovereign, and this often did not reflect the metal content. Precious metal as the ideal form of money is refuted by the impracticality of the coinage. The high value of pure gold or silver coins meant that they were not useful for most daily purposes, and their soft nature made them open to shaving. Despite the association of money with gold, most of the earliest coinage was mainly silver or silver-alloy. The basic coin was a 'silver penny'. It was a small, thin disc of metal of uncertain quality. However, as the European economies started to grow rulers found it hard to keep enough coinage circulating, given the limited amounts of metal available.

Even when silver and gold coins circulated widely, such as across Europe during the reign of Charlemagne, it was still a coinage for the elite rather than the mass of the people, who used base-metal coins or other records of debts and payments such as tabs (a written or verbal record), notched sticks (tallies – Box 3.2) or personal trust. Even for state use such as payment of taxes, the more mundane forms of money, particularly tallies, were predominant. When the king was in his counting house he was as likely to be counting tally sticks as coin. China also had tally sticks made of bamboo as early as 1046 BCE. So, even when the use of gold and silver was at its height, other forms of money were widely in use.

Box 3.2: Tally sticks

Tally sticks were short lengths of flat wood. The agreed payment would be carved into the wood by cutting different sizes of grooves across the stick to represent the actual amount. On the reverse of the stick the names of the two parties would be written. The stick was then cut into two lengthways and the debtor and creditor would each take a half. Where the debtor was considered creditworthy their tally-stick IOU could circulate as money. The tally sticks could be seen as an early version of a cheque book: the two halves of the stick were called the stub or foil and the stock.

In Britain the late 1600s were a period of intense political debate about the nature of money. While some argued that paper and base-metal money should be recognised as the main circulating medium, others argued to retain the intrinsic nature of money by maintaining the link to precious metal. A major exponent of the need to root money in precious metal was the philosopher John Locke (1632–1704). As a liberal he was concerned about the role of the monarchy in the control of money and saw the precious-metal link as a way of anchoring an independent money. This motivation lies behind modern innovations such as cryptocurrency that aim to set up an autonomous money system, as discussed in Chapter Six.

John Locke's view prevailed, and the decision was made that all the metal currency would be re-coined to make the face-value equivalent to the precious-metal content. This led to a chronic shortage of coin, with the added problem that gold and silver continually fluctuated in price. When the price of gold and silver went up, people melted down the coins to sell the bullion. When the price of bullion went down, the coinage lost value. The problem of stabilising the coinage was left in the hands of the governor of the Royal Mint. In 1717 this was the scientist Isaac Newton. His aim was to stabilise the weight of gold and silver that the coins should contain. Up to that time most British coinage had been made of silver, but over the next century gold became predominant. The area in which the standardisation of value became most important was the relationship between the newly emerging form of money, banknotes, and their value in precious metal.

As will be described in the next chapter, banknotes became increasingly important in the circulation of money. As Adam Smith noted, in Scotland by the early 1700s paper money represented three-quarters of circulating money. The problem was, how did the various forms of paper money compare with the ideal of precious-metal money? What were the paper promises emerging from the banks worth? The early banknotes were a 'promise to pay on demand'. What should the bank pay? The fairy tale that sees the solution in the use of commodity money does not help because the price (value) of commodities fluctuates. What became known as the gold standard aimed to answer this problem by fixing the amount of gold that each note would represent. Far from being a feature of the market, the 'price' of money was to be set by the monetary authority of the state.

In Britain the attempt to link the new forms of money, particularly paper, to a fixed standard had a mixed outcome. It proved problematic in times of national crisis, particularly war, when much more money was needed. This was overcome by suspending the gold standard for periods of time. Although it lasted until the twentieth century and saw long periods of price stability, the gold standard also caused economic problems. Winston Churchill's putting Britain back on the gold standard at a high rate in 1925 is seen as a major contribution to the severity of the Depression in the 1930s.

Britain finally came off the gold standard in 1931, and the US stopped exchanging currency for gold to anyone except central banks in 1933. This final central bank 'window' was abolished in 1973. Since then, leading currencies have generally floated against each other, apart from in experiments such as the European Exchange Rate Mechanism (ERM), which Britain spectacularly exited in 1992 when the pound could not maintain its prescribed value against the other currencies. The ERM was largely superseded by the euro.

The main impact of the gold standard wasn't within countries but between counties. Currencies fixed their international value in terms of gold, at first through the pound and latterly, following the Bretton Woods agreement of 1944, through the dollar at the rate of $35 dollars an ounce. Although the notional link with gold was maintained for nearly four hundred years, its high point as the basis for interaction between currencies operated most effectively from the second half of the nineteenth century to the First World War. However, this may not have been the result of the gold standard, but of the economic dominance of the British economy in that period, to be replaced by the dominance of the American economy in the twentieth century. It was not the holdings of gold that drove economic activity, it was the circulation of trusted paper, the pound sterling and the dollar. This becomes more clearly the case in the present era of fiat public currencies.

Since the early 1970s there is no pretence of any superior form of money backing the circulating currency, whether it is notes, coin or electronic records. So what gives money its validity now? Why do people trust and use money? The fairy story of money has proved to be unhelpful and the long experiment with gold has proved to be flawed. The alternative is to see all money forms as having validity through a combination of authority and trust. It is not some inherent economic value that drives money. Money is a social and political construct. It rests on the trust of the people in each other to honour the metal coins, paper, shells, electronic transfers or whatever passes for money, in their daily lives.

I argued in the previous chapter that similarities could be found between the uses of money in traditional communities and its use today. A similar question can be asked of the sovereign power to create and control money. Given that markets are so prevalent, what is the current role of the state in relation to the creation and circulation of money? Is handbag economics correct? Has the state diminished to the status of a household, dependent on the market to deliver prosperity? If so, when did the transition occur from the powerful monetary control of Alexander the Great to the imposition of neoliberal austerity on the state today? The answer lies in the critical interaction between money and taxation.

Sovereign money: tribute and tax

The importance of coin in the payment of taxes is captured in the Bible. Jesus is set a trap by being asked whether a coin should be used to pay taxes imposed by the Romans on the Jews. He asks whose face is on the coin. It is Caesar's. In that historical period the coin could have been a Roman denarius featuring the emperor Tiberius, also known as the 'tribute penny'. Jesus avoids the trap by acknowledging the link between money and state: 'Render therefore unto Caesar the things which be Caesar's.'[3]

Taxation has a long history. China has records of taxation going back three thousand years. As a concept it seems to imply an onerous payment to someone with the power to make that demand. 'Taxing' is a word used to describe a difficult activity. 'Tax' appeared as a word in English in the fourteenth century and could have derived from the Latin *taxare*, meaning to 'evaluate, estimate, assess'. Taxation has been the source of political rebellion throughout history, from the Barons who forced the signing of Magna Carta in 1215, to the poll tax riots of 1381 (and their repeat in 1982), to the Boston Tea Party in 1773. All seem to imply that taxation is a bad thing.

Early civilisations (5000 BCE) carried into them the social hierarchies that existed in non-market societies. This combined the power to demand a contribution from the populace of the emerging city-state (tax, tribute) with the requirement to redistribute (allocation, payment). This required standards for measurement and comparison. One of the earliest value symbols was grain. As we have seen, as civilisations developed they adopted a range of money forms. These did not emerge from the market and were not handed down by tradition; they were adopted or created consciously by rulers. Taxation and other public payments can be seen as playing a major role in this.

As we have seen, in pre-modern societies tribute, injury and social payments were the main uses for money. In the emerging civilisations, sovereign money was widely used for war. For empires such as Rome, citizens might escape being taxed, as resources, labour and wealth could be extracted from conquered populations. However, some military adventures were hugely expensive. The many crusades launched to take back Jerusalem from its Muslim rulers required large amounts of money. In 1188–89 a 'Saladin' tithe (Saladin was the Muslim ruler of Jerusalem) raised the equivalent of more than two years' total income for the British Crown through a land tax, known as a 'tallage'. This is thought to have given rise to two words, 'tallies' – that is, the tally sticks on which payment was recorded – and 'tellers', the officers who collected the tax. In Britain the coordination of taxes was through the Exchequer, first established in Anglo Saxon times between 991 and 1012. The name is thought to refer to a large table covered with a cloth patterned in squares like a chess board, on which payment for goods received by the state and taxes paid to the state were set out.

There are different ways in which a ruler can obtain the things that they need. One is to demand taxes in kind: payment in goods, labour or resources. Another is to pay with the coins of the realm. Where the ruler controls the issue and circulation of money s/he can exercise seigniorage. This can be direct or indirect. The indirect approach is to demand a fee from private citizens for the right to mint coins. In the late 900s the kings of Wessex in Britain had several hundred 'moneyers', individuals licensed to create coins subject to a payment to the Crown. Every five or six years the king would declare the coins invalid and they would have to be handed in, to be re-issued with another payment to the Crown for the privilege. The direct approach is for the ruler to control the mints and to have the benefit of the first use of the new money.

The two ways of raising tax are very different. In the first case the production of money is in private hands and the ruler extracts some of that money as tax. In the second version the ruler controls the production of money and the task of taxation is to reclaim that money so that it can be re-spent. I will argue in the final chapter of this book that these two very different relationships between the creation of money and taxation still exist. The first is private creation of money, some of which is acquired by the state through taxation. The second is public creation of money, some or all of which is retrieved by the state through taxation. The latter model of state-generated money is more transparent if we look at the use of tally sticks as acknowledgement of public expenditure (Box 3.3).

Box 3.3: Paying tax in tally sticks

A merchant supplies the ruler with goods. The ruler gives the merchant a tally stick acknowledging receipt and the value of the goods. The merchant presents the tally stick to the Exchequer (Treasury) in lieu of paying tax. If the tally stick value exceeds the amount of tax due, the merchant will receive another tally stick for the remaining amount. The merchant will use this tally stick to make a payment to another trader who needs the tally stick to pay tax. Tally sticks were used extensively for the payment of tax in Britain until the 1820s.

In this example the origin of the money form clearly starts with the ruler. The issue of the tally stick starts the transfer process. The stick is either returned as a tax or circulated so that another taxpayer can meet their obligation. Taxation is, therefore, a major way of making money circulate. In the broadly subsistence economies of the previous chapter there was little need for circulating money. As we have seen, it was when money taxation was imposed that people were forced to seek out sources of the relevant money.

Taxation makes people accept whatever the money form is in payment for their labour, goods or services, as they need it to pay their taxes. The importance of this dynamic role of taxation does not depend on a particular type of money such as silver or gold. Whatever form of money the state demands in payment of taxes must be the one people must seek out. In this context, a particular money does not create the basis for taxation, but taxation creates the necessity for a particular money. The nature of money is not determined by the market or the material of which it is made; it is determined by the state itself.

The central role of taxation in the creation and circulation of money was put forward in the early twentieth century by the German Georg Knapp (1842–1926). In his major work *The State Theory of Money*, Knapp argues that money is not an economic phenomenon linked to the market; it is very much a public phenomenon, 'a creature of law'.[4] For this reason, he sees the study of the monetary system as a branch of political science rather than economics. It is the state that establishes the status of money forms such as coins or public currency notes. Far from having intrinsic value or being seen as deriving from such a value, Knapp sees money as a token that he calls a 'chartal' (Latin for token), whose value is defined by the local context.

He notes that the first question a trader will ask in a new country is, what is the nature of the currency? He also points to the social and public use of money, such as fees and fines as well as taxes. Knapp sees such public administrative payments as a better grounding for the existence of money than the notion that money originated in trade. He acknowledges that commodities such as precious metal have been used in exchange, but he does not consider this to be adequate as money. For Knapp the means of transfer and measurement only becomes money proper when it has no intrinsic value. Although paper money was well established at the time Knapp was writing, he wanted to establish its status as a public currency. He argued that paper or other non-material money is not inferior to metal money, all are part of an administrative monetary system.[5]

Knapp's state theory of money and the exercise of the sovereign power to create money has a very different emphasis to fairy-tale economic thinking. The myth of money as originating and circulating in markets is refuted by the long history of the monetary role of states. Sovereign control over the creation and circulation of money enabled rulers to build economic and political power. However, this was not unlimited. Rulers could authorise or issue only as much money as the economy could bear and the taxation system could reclaim. The power of the sovereign rests in the willingness or coercion of people to give up their labour, resources, even their lives for a token.

Seeing states as the source of money leads to a very different view of taxation from conventional economics. Perspectives such as neoliberal handbag economics see taxation as extracting money from the wealth developed in the market-place. This money is then spent back into circulation through public spending. The alternative view sees the sovereign creating and spending money into circulation when buying goods and services. By spending this money the sovereign acquires the goods and services required. The function of taxation is to ask for that money back again. The need to pay their taxes would be the reason people would accept and circulate the designated sovereign money.

While in the latter approach the creation and circulation of money precedes taxation, the underlying resource that lies behind that money is the power of the sovereign to extract goods, services and resources from the people. This power can certainly be coercive and corrupt. However, where sovereign power rests with the people, as is at least theoretically the case in modern democracies, the use of publicly issued money can be seen as enabling people to provide labour, goods and services for themselves as citizens. This case will be made in the final chapter.

This chapter has drawn attention to the extensive involvement of states in the production and circulation of money over a long historical period. The important role of public monetary authorities is still evident. No nation allows the minting of coin or the printing of money without authorisation. All nations have central banks and exercise public monetary authority to a greater or lesser extent. Historically, rulers have exercised sovereign power over the creation and circulation of money. Today in democracies sovereign power rests, at least in theory, with the people or their representatives. Yet currently the public ability to create and circulate money is not seen as legitimate. Modern currencies are public but not sovereign. So, who does have the power to create and circulate public currencies, and on whose authority? The answer is in the next chapter.

FOUR

Conjuring money out of thin air: money and banking

A classic magician's trick is to conjure an object out of thin air. The audience is shown an empty container. With the tap of a wand or a dramatic flourish, the container now contains an object such as a bottle or a bunch of flowers. This chapter will show how banks can do the same thing with money and, more specifically, the public currency. The public currency is the authorised yardstick and means of transfer of notional value in a monetary community, usually a nation-state. As we saw in the previous chapter, public currencies are strongly identified with rulers and centres of power.

Unlike with the traditional forms of money in Chapter Two, whose origin is generally unknown, rulers such as Alexander the Great and Charlemagne consciously created and named their chosen currency. We also saw how Chinese rulers set up new money systems, including some based upon paper. Public currency is therefore not just coin. It is anything the ruling authority declares to be money that the people accept and use.

The emergence of modern banking in the fourteenth century saw two new additions to the family of money things: banknotes and bank accounts. This chapter will explain how these became synonymous with the public currency. The process is illustrated by the banknotes discussed in the Introduction and Chapter One.

The dollar bill, the pound note and the euro note look superficially the same. They are each based on numbers: one dollar, five pounds, ten euros. They all operate in the same way. They are fiat money. None is convertible into any other form of money, other than into another currency (euros to dollars,

dollars to pounds). The money is not valuable in itself. It is just a piece of paper. When held in a bank account the dollar, pound or euro is not even a piece of paper. Yet it works as money all the same. It is used as a standard measure for comparing value and as a means of transferring that value from account to account.

Despite their similarities, differences between the currency notes reveal the way control of public currencies has passed from the era of rulers to the era of banks. As discussed in the last chapter, precious-metal money was strongly associated with rulers and military and political power. To this day, most states retain control over the minting of coin. This history is embodied in the modern pound note. It declares that it promises to pay the bearer the sum of five, ten or twenty pounds, assumed to be in the form of precious metal. Although pound banknotes are now clearly seen as the public currency, even described as cash as opposed to a bank account, the words on the note imply that this is a promise of money, not money in itself. The history of bank-created money is the story of how paper promises became the public currency.

The history of the dollar is quite different. It has its origins in government-created paper money. It makes no claim to be exchangeable for another form of money and the authority of the state is shown by its declared status as 'legal tender'. The dollar is money because the state says it is. In the case of the euro, I have argued that it is simply a mechanism of measurement and transfer. It only states its monetary units – five, ten, twenty. It mentions neither governments nor banks. It promises nothing, gives no instruction and does not name an issuer. It seems to come from nowhere. I will look at the euro more closely in Chapter Six.

Myths and fairy tales about banks

According to the fairy tale in Box 1.1, banks originated in the need to have somewhere to safely keep precious-metal money. Over time, the banks began to make loans based on those cash deposits. One major myth about banking derives from this story: that the main activity of banks is to link savers and borrowers. This implies that banks can lend out only money that they have previously received either as saving accounts (where money is deposited, often for a fixed amount of time) or as current accounts where the content of the account is not fixed and money is constantly being deposited and withdrawn as people go about their daily business.

The logic of this myth must be that if someone has been given a loan by the bank the money must be drawn from existing saving or current bank accounts. If the assertion that banks merely link savers and borrowers is correct, as illustrated in the cartoon, the money to pay for the house purchase must be taken from bank deposits and will not be fully replaced until the end of twenty-five years. As the cartoon shows, the granting of mortgage loans does not strip other bank accounts of their money.

Bank loans don't affect existing deposits

What, then, are bank loans based on? The answer is nothing but the perceived viability of the bank. As with the story of money in general, the story of banking is riddled with myths and half-truths. While the story that bank lending is based on bank deposits proves not to be the case, there is some truth in the tale's description of the role of banks in the security of cash and the development of non-coin forms of money, banknotes and bank accounts.

Some people did deposit money for safe keeping, and the receipts they were given in exchange were so trusted that they were used widely as paper money. Deposits of coin and other valuables were mainly related to long-distance travel by traders and military campaigners. This required equally long-distance networks of bankers. An early example is the Knights Templar (Box 4.1).

Box 4.1: The Knights Templar money network

The Knights Templar were an order of warrior monks who undertook the task of safeguarding the pilgrims joining the Crusades to the Holy Land, the first of which took place in 1099. The pilgrims needed money to fund their journey and for the time they would spend in Jerusalem. Networks of Knights Templar monks arranged the transport of money and the settlement of payments and debts along the route of the Crusades. Pilgrims would leave cash at the Knights' Temple church in London and withdraw an equivalent sum when in Jerusalem. Their deposit would be acknowledged by a letter of credit to be presented to the Templars in Jerusalem.

The Templars also made loans. In the 1200s the British crown jewels were lodged at the Templars' London Temple church as security for a loan to the monarch. Philip IV of France was so indebted to the Templars that he attacked their Paris Temple in 1307, tortured the monks and burned the grandmaster to death. The Knights Templar Order was disbanded in 1312 after the Christian crusaders lost control of Jerusalem.

Like the sovereign-controlled money discussed in the previous chapter, the emergence of the modern banking system was closely linked to war and conquest. Several hundred years after the Knights Templar banking network was established, another major conflict helped to create the Rothschild banking empire. Like the Templars, the Rothschilds formed a network of bankers, this time based on five brothers, each in a different city (London, Frankfurt, Paris, Vienna, Naples). This arrangement allowed money to be transferred safely across Europe and was a vital resource to the British during the Napoleonic Wars.

The examples of the Knights Templar and the Rothschilds show important aspects of a bank's work. Two major activities of banks are managing accounts and making loans. Managing accounts involves activities such as money changing and the transfer of money between people or on behalf of clients across different monetary boundaries. This requires accounting and record keeping, often with written notes authorising payments. Loans are also a major activity, again with paper records of loan obligations. The main forms of bank papers were bills of trading and promissory notes. Bills of trading allowed money to be paid in one location for the delivery of goods in another location. Promissory notes were statements of a debt owed. These early paper records were based on different amounts of money, depending on the circumstances – that is, they recorded the actual value of the loan or deposit.

The first standardised banknotes, naming a fixed sum, were issued by the Bank of Sweden in Stockholm, which was founded in 1657 as a joint venture between an entrepreneur and the monarchy. The banknotes promised to pay the bearer the specified sum in precious metal. As in the fairy story, the bank issued more notes than it had metal and the bank collapsed. This pattern was to be repeated. The desire to have a 'sound base' for money succumbed to the reality that more money was always needed than precious-metal money could provide.

The fairy tale assumption that precious metal was the original and ideal form of money meant that the new paper money was seen merely as a record of banking activity and, as such, it was not 'real' money. As we have seen, this assumption led to the prolonged attempt to maintain a link between cash (originally coin, later also Bank of England notes) and gold. The weakness of these assumptions lies in the much larger amount of paper money in circulation than is justified by deposits of 'real' money. If paper money is meant to directly reflect cash deposits and banks merely act as a link between savers and borrowers, the only conclusion must be that somewhere in the system there is cheating. This is where the concept of 'fractional reserve banking' appears to put forward an explanation that avoids this charge.

'Fractional reserve banking' starts from the premise that not everyone wants to take out the money they have deposited in the bank at the same time. It is therefore perfectly acceptable for the bank to lend some of it out (Box 4.2). Fractional reserve banking usually assumes a ratio of 10:1. The bank must retain in ready money a sum equivalent to 10% of the money lent. This allows a growth of paper money in relation to the original deposit, which is assumed to be 'real' money.

Box 4.2: Fractional reserve banking

Lady 1 makes a deposit in her bank account of £10-worth of gold coins. The banker gives her a £10 paper receipt. The bank then keeps 10% and lends £9-worth of the gold coin to Lady 2, holding £1-worth of the coin in reserve. Lady 2 deposits the £9 of gold coin in her account and gets a paper receipt worth £9. Her bank then lends £8.10-worth of the gold coin to Lady 3 and holds 90p in reserve. Lady 3 puts the £8.10 of gold coin into her account and gets a paper receipt, and so on. Already we have £27-worth of paper receipts but only £10-worth of gold coin.

It is clear that the model of fractional reserve banking is fundamentally unstable. Yet it is the principle on which Western banking has been founded. The security of the whole system rests on the notion of a small amount of reserves 'backing' all the accounts in circulation and that people will not panic and want all their money back at once.

The notion of fractional reserve banking therefore sees banks as being in a position where they have made a promise to depositors that they can always get their money back on demand, while lending out much larger amounts of money that will be paid back over time with interest. This makes the bank very profitable if nothing goes wrong. However, banks are open to a liquidity crisis if all the money is demanded back at the same time by the depositors. The loans are generally long term, as compared to the deposits, which are always open to short-term demand. The banks face a crisis of solvency if the loans are likely to turn bad and never be repaid.

Fractional reserve banking means that banks are always vulnerable to a 'run'. As this did happen on a regular basis, the solution involved the intervention of the state through the formation of central banks to stabilise the situation, as will be explained below. However, this only pushed the problem back to the inadequacy of reserves of precious metal at the central bank, as the experience of the gold standard discussed in the last chapter showed. A mythology that there is such a thing as 'real' money is therefore highly destabilising. People expect there to be something real behind the money system. They will always be disappointed with such an illusion as there is nothing at the heart of money but social trust and public authority. Modern money in particular is a network of promises that have become the public currency.

A different kind of magic

An alternative analysis of the development of bank-created money challenges the mythical history of precious-metal bank deposits and spurious loans. Far from modern money emerging from precious-metal banking, it can be seen as originating in the paper promises and bank accounts themselves. Rather than a role in safeguarding precious-metal money, the role of the bank was much more to do with the requirements of trade. Two important elements characterise this view of banking activities: credit-debt and clearing. Credit-debt is making a promise of future payment (Box 4.3). Clearing is the tallying of credit-debt promises. Credit-debt is so called because the borrower has the benefit of access to a transferrable form of money or some other benefit now (credit) in return for a commitment to return that money or pay for that benefit later (debt).

Box 4.3: Trade and credit-debt

A trader goes to a weaver for a roll of cloth to sell on his travels. They agree a price. As the trader does not have any cash to buy the cloth, he promises the weaver that he will pay the agreed price on his return. The trader gives the weaver a note confirming this promise. As the weaver cannot wait until the trader returns she takes the trader's promise to someone who is wealthy enough to take the risk of the trader not returning. To compensate the risk-taker, she is paid less than the value of the original debt (a discount).

The risk-taker could pay the weaver for the trader's promise in the recognised currency. This would have validity through the authority of the sovereign. However, the risk-taker could give the weaver a substitute promise to pay. Because the risk-taker is widely trusted, the weaver can then use the risk-taker's promissory note to buy goods and services from another trader. This would be honoured because of the perceived credibility of the person or institution making the promise to pay.

From the late 1600s banks began to circulate their own currency in the form of standardised banknotes bearing the individual name of the bank. These bank 'promises to pay' circulated as money because bank promises were more credit-worthy than personal promises. A private agreement between traders would not qualify as money unless that promise could be transferred readily. What the banks were doing was taking on the risk of private promises by putting the banks' own credit in their place, pending future payment. The same process is the basis of banking today. For example, if someone is buying a car he could pay cash, but more likely he will use a cheque or a card payment. The seller of the car will let the buyer drive away with the vehicle not because she trusts the buyer, but she trusts the buyer's bank to honour the payment. The bank then takes the risk that the buyer will have enough credit in the bank, or the credit-worthiness to pay the debt to the bank eventually. It is this network of credit and debt that explains the amount of paper money in circulation, not the existence of original cash deposits.

Clearing: sorting promises

Central to a bank's activities is the process of 'clearing' whereby networks of credit-debt promises are tallied against each other (Box 4.4).

Box 4.4: Promissory notes

Mary owes Jim £100 and gives him a promissory note that the money will be paid in due course.

Jim owes Carol £100 and asks her if she will accept Mary's promissory note to settle the debt.

Carol owes Mary £100 so she agrees with Mary that she will just tear up Mary's promissory note so that Mary no longer has to pay Jim £100. This also settles Carol's debt to Mary.

All debts are now paid.

This process of cancelling debts against each other means that actual payments are relatively smaller than the total amount of monetary obligations in circulation. The process of clearing happens within a bank, but also between banks.

If clearing and final settlement payments are being made within the same bank an internal transfer can take place between account holders. However, if a payment drawn on an account in Bank A is paid into Bank B, Bank A needs to transfer the equivalent amount of money into Bank B. As cross-payments between banks can also cancel each other out, once again, the clearing process leaves a much smaller amount needing to be transferred for settlement.

The new institutions of banking based on promises to pay contravened one of the oldest of moral injunctions: against debt and the payment of interest. Exploitative lending at interest (usury) was a major concern of most religions and widely condemned. Historically, debt was often associated with the uncertainties of farming, requiring loans of grain or of domesticated animals. Rulers often intervened when debts got too high and declared debt jubilees, cancelling all debts. Bankers and other people engaged in money lending were often vilified, yet debt became the basis of modern money. Modern market capitalism could not exist without access to credit-debt in advance of production and trade. In the process, credit-debt networks changed the structure of society.

The rich bewitched: debt becomes a way of life

From the time of the Knights Templar there was a steady growth of commercial banking. Italy was foremost, led by the great trading cities of Venice, Florence and Genoa. The Medici family set up their first bank in 1397. Over the next two hundred years banking became established across Europe. As pointed out earlier, the word 'bank' is thought to stem from the Italian for bench, *banco*. Money changers, lenders and deposit holders would sit at small tables in major trading centres. Like the Knights Templar, they formed networks across countries and markets, sometimes using their own private currencies. Merchants could deposit or borrow money in one centre and then draw money in another city or country. The network of bankers would periodically get together and 'clear' all the credit notes and settle any remaining debts.

Modern banking emerged as Europe was beginning the process of consolidation into what would become nation-states. Disputed land was the basis of local wars, skirmishes, fortifications and standing armies. This cost a lot of money and local rulers often exhausted their treasuries, as there was a limit to how much public currency money could be retrieved in taxes. Rulers started to turn to the new private sources of money through taking out loans from the growing body of bankers. Repayment was often funded through some form of tax or the granting of a trading monopoly or licence to the lender.

Like the Knights Templar, Italian bankers made loans to rulers. The relationship was a close one: early Italian bankers such as the Medici family linked economic, military and political power. However, rulers could default, and many of the early banks were ruined. As will be explained below, the failure of successive monarchs to pay their debts led to the creation of the Bank of England and the establishment of a 'national debt'. However, it was not just the monarchs who became embroiled in the new form of promissory money.

The advent of bank-issued paper promises saw a marked change in the lives of the aristocratic elites. Traditionally their wealth had come in the feudal form of direct labour or payment of rents. With the new credit-debt money they could monetise their capital wealth. Like rulers, they could issue promises to pay, using the value of their lands or their future income as collateral. One consequence of this seemingly easy money was a craze for gambling and high living generally. By the 1800s the aristocracy across Europe were widely engaged in gambling. It had become a key activity in social gatherings. Reckless gambling was an indicator of wealth and social status and relieved the boredom of the leisured ruling class. However, betting by the subordinate classes was widely banned.

Aristocrats found that bankers were eager to lend them paper and other forms of money. Alternatively, landed elites paid creditors and tradesmen with promises in the form of bonds (promises to pay a specific sum at a future date) or annuities. Annuities are agreements to pay a regular sum of money over a period of time, rather than settle a debt immediately. Major gamblers such as the Whig politician Charles James Fox could lose or win thousands of pounds in one sitting, and people could lose their entire fortune in one night. Another profligate gambler was Georgiana Cavendish, Duchess of Devonshire (1757–1806). Georgiana was a charismatic and beautiful woman. She was a socialite and political activist for the anti-monarchist Whig party as well as being a novelist and promoter of Enlightenment science. With her husband, the Duke of Devonshire, she gambled away most of what had been one of the largest fortunes in Britain.

While the new promise to pay in paper money made debt a way of life, a radical experiment took place in France that was based on a different kind of promise. The promise was not a debt on the part of a borrower, but the promise of a credit. The Scotsman John Law aimed to create a new form of paper money that promised future wealth for the holder.

The John Law experiment

John Law (1671–1729) was born in Scotland to a family of goldsmiths and bankers. Like many of the wealthy men of his age, he was a gambler and a dandy, killing a love rival in a duel. He escaped punishment by fleeing across the Channel, eventually returning to Scotland. In 1705 Law put forward his idea that, rather than people issuing private notes of credit-debt using their land as collateral, the state itself should provide paper credits through a national bank backed by tangible assets such as land, gold and silver and the productivity of the nation.

Law argued that money was not something that was, or should be, valuable in itself. The real wealth was in trade and industry. Paper money should represent that value, like share certificates represent the value of a company. His ideas were rejected in England but taken up in France, where the young king was sorely in need of funds. The wars fought by the previous monarch, Louis XIV, had left the country bankrupt, with a severe shortage of precious metal. After Louis XIV's death the regency for the young Louis XV was open to new ideas.

Rather than his initial proposal to set up a national bank, in 1716 Law set up a private bank, the Banque Générale, that issued paper banknotes whose value was ultimately based on the promise of riches from the French overseas territory of Louisiana. The new money was effectively share certificates in the potential wealth of the Mississippi region and the promise of future tax income.

In 1719 Law issued 50,000 new shares with a face-value of 500 livres which people could purchase for only 75 livres, paying the rest in instalments. This led to a boom in the value of the shares. Before the next instalment was due the value of the shares doubled to 1,000 livres. Law then issued another 300,000 shares on the same basis. The total number of shares then rose to 600,000 and the share value shot up to 15,000 livres. People clamoured for the shares and borrowed extensively to buy them. It became a classic bubble.

The scramble for the share-money created such a surge of apparent wealth that in 1720 Law was made Controller General of the Finances of France. However, problems quickly surfaced. Releasing so much money into the economy led to inflation. As with all such booms, as confidence evaporated, people found their share-money collapsing in value. The lack of any real wealth behind the promises became obvious as people tried to 'cash in' their banknotes. People protested in the streets and attacked financiers. Law was sacked from his post within the year.

Although Law's scheme collapsed, he had stumbled upon a truth about money. Money did not need to be scarce or valuable in itself. In fact, paper money could expand economies much more quickly than the restrictive gold/silver money. In the first two years his method worked and internal and external trade grew dramatically. However, rather than using the paper money to expand economic activities, people saw the money as an asset in itself, expecting it to continually grow in value. As was the experience with gold, money is more useful when it is not valuable in itself.

Sovereign money and bank money

Although coinage was the main early form of money in Europe, rulers were increasingly less able to exert the control that the early empires such as those of Alexander and the Romans displayed.

The invention of precious-metal coinage was a huge boost to sovereign power, particularly in the payment of mercenaries, but it was also a weakness. Precious-metal coinage had a paradoxical effect because, although it was very much a public institution, dominated by rulers, the rulers depended on access to the metal which was often in the hands of traders and adventurers. Rulers still controlled the process of coining, so that when traders brought in the raw metal (bullion) to be melted into coin they were charged a fee.

The balance of value between coin and bullion was delicate. There was always the danger that people would prefer to extract the precious metal from the coins, if the commodity price went too high, causing a dramatic shortage of coinage. For this reason, debased coin was often more useful. Most early coins did not have values on their faces; the value of each coin was announced by the ruling authorities. This allowed rulers to 'cry up' or 'cry down' the value of their coinage.

The need to guarantee the value of metal coinage led to the formation of one of the first central banks, the Bank of Amsterdam in 1609. The new bank took over the role of coinage minting from a range of private coiners. At the time, Holland had two forms of coinage: high-quality coins for external trade and inferior coins for internal use. As both were prone to damage and tarnishing, the bank took in the coin and registered it as a credit in its books. People started to exchange this credit rather than deal with the coin. However, it was not until 1668 that the first paper banknotes were issued, when the Bank of Sweden became the first central bank to issue banknotes in standardised denominations that could be circulated as public currency. This marked an important transition between the private commercial circulation of paper promises and an authorised paper currency.

As discussed in the last chapter, in England this led to a debate about the efficacy of adopting an official paper money, but the idea was rejected. It would be over a hundred years before the British state established its monopoly over the creation of this form of money through the Bank of England. The history of the Bank of England, like much of the relationship between rulers and the new bank lenders, was rooted in the expense of war. In the late 1600s King William III needed to borrow additional money to fight the French. This was not readily forthcoming, as the monarchy had a bad credit rating because of earlier defaults by the Stuart kings.

In 1694 a group of merchants led by William Paterson came together to form a privately owned Bank of England that would provide the king with a loan of £1.2 million on which interest of 8% per annum would be paid. The king could draw on this sum in the bank's promissory banknotes, the bank's 'promise to pay'. As the money made available to the king was to be returned, the bank used this as an asset against which it issued another £1.2 million-worth of banknotes to be lent to non-state borrowers. To ensure that the king would fulfil his commitment to repay the money, the new bank demanded that the loan should be guaranteed by Parliament.

This was no longer a private credit-debt relationship between banker and ruler, it was now a privately funded loan to the ruler guaranteed by the citizens. It had become a national debt, a commitment in the name of the people. This would be the case for all future lending to the state: it was all consolidated as the national debt. Even when the Bank of England was made responsible for issuing the national currency, and eventually nationalised, there was no return to the idea of state-controlled money. The state became a borrower like everybody else. The state could no longer control the creation and circulation of the national currency directly and exercise seigniorage, the benefit of first use of new money.

With its two sets of banknote loans, the Bank of England straddled public and commercial lending. It was a private commercial organisation with a public remit, making loans available to the state. At the same time, the burgeoning capitalist market economy needed a constant supply of cheap credit. As Law had noted, coinage, particularly precious-metal coinage, was not sufficiently fluid and flexible enough for the new age. Mundane forms of transfer such as tallies and banknotes were more useful.

The transition from private promises to bank-generated public currency now began to take place. The privately created credit-debt 'promise to pay' banknotes over time *became* the public currency. As commercial credit expanded, the integration of private and public money was enhanced by private banks starting to open accounts with the Bank of England and use its banknotes. This became formalised in 1833 when a Bank Charter Act gave the still privately owned Bank of England a monopoly on the creation of banknotes. The Bank Charter Act of 1844 sought to anchor the creation of Bank of England banknotes to the level of precious metal that it held, but this did not limit the creation of bank accounts. The Bank of England was finally nationalised in 1946.

As pointed out earlier, the Bank of England banknote formally retains the implication that it is linked to some superior form of money. The note promises to pay the bearer the amount stated on the note. The note itself does not claim to be money, it appears to be promising payment of 'real' money, taken to be precious-metal coin. As we have seen, this distinction between 'real' money and inferior forms stems from the European obsession with precious metal. Other countries such as China and the US were much more flexible about the forms that money could take, both having adopted state paper money. In contrast, the British state fought long and hard in a failed attempt to tie its paper money to precious metal. Today the bearer presenting a banknote to the Bank of England would just get another note in its place.

The confusion between the state's sovereign power to create money and the ability of banks to create paper notes is most notable in the history of the United States. Although the US developed as a market society with a culture of rugged individualism and limited governance from its inception, it also has a public history including the creation of state paper money. State-created money funded the War of Independence from 1775 to the early 1780s and played a major role in the Civil War of 1861–65. However, while the US Constitution explicitly granted the right to create coined money to Congress (Article I, Section 8, Clause 5), the position for paper money was less clear. This left open whether the paper money should be fiat money created and circulated by the state, or bank-issued paper money created through bank loans.

As commercial banks sprang up across the US, the aim seems to have been to restrict their power by keeping them local, confined within state boundaries, rather than regulating them at federal level. However, this did not stop problems of over-indebtedness, particularly of farmers, and the fragility of bank solvency. Without a central bank there was an unregulated free-for-all and many banks collapsed. Finally, in 1907 a major crisis was caused by a panic that started in the stock market but caused a run on a number of banks which had lent money to investors. The panic was stopped by the banker J.P. Morgan, whose credit-worthiness was sufficient to give people confidence to trust their banks. In 1913 the major banks got together to set up a federal reserve bank (The Fed) to undertake the role of a central bank.

As fiat money, the efficacy of contemporary public currencies is based on a mixture of social trust, public authority and commercial confidence. In sustaining a public currency, central banks are the bridge between the banking sector and the state. Central banks, as an arm of the state, share the state's prerogative of creating and spending money directly. As we will see in the next chapter, this capacity was demonstrated following the financial crisis of 2007–08, when central banks created new electronic money to support their banking sectors. Central banks are both a banker for the state and a banker for the banks. As a banker for the state, central banks manage state accounts and underwrite state spending. As a banker to the banking sector, they act as clearing banks to settle accounts between the different banks and underwrite bank lending. This is often expressed as being 'a lender of last resort'. If necessary, the central bank can provide unlimited amounts of money. It is the ultimate magic money tree.

How the trick is done

How, then, do banks create money?

What modern banks cannot do is create their own banknotes and coin. That remains the prerogative of the monetary authorities. What banks can create is a bank loan that puts new numbers of the public currency units (pounds, dollars, euros) into a bank account. It is this money which is magical, conjured out of nowhere. The bank declares the money to be available and transferrable and everyone accepts that that is the case. The loan provides the borrower with immediate access to the money, with an obligation to pay it back with interest by the agreed date.

If the whole process of borrowing, spending and repaying the money is done through bank accounts there is no need to involve any state-issued money such as banknotes and coin. If the borrower does demand cash the bank uses its own reserves of notes and coin or buys additional cash from the Bank of England, paying with money drawn from the bank's account at the Bank of England. In today's Britain most money is in the form of bank accounts, existing only as a record. Only about 3% is represented by cash (notes and coin). As people use less and less cash, bank-account money is the main mechanism of transfer.

Banks did not plan to be able to create the public currency through their lending. There was no conspiracy of bankers. Banks started out by creating their own paper promises as well as dealing in various coinages. Over time, commercial-promise money and state-regulated public currency merged. This is illustrated most clearly by the British pound note. It started as a private promise to pay that, over time, became so trusted that it became the public currency. The commercial creation of paper money gained the authority of the state. Banknotes came to be treated as if they were coins. Later, state guarantee of bank-generated money extended to bank accounts as well as paper money.

This did not resolve the conundrum of fractional reserve banking. Banks still created many more loans than they had assets, no longer issuing them as banknotes but setting them up as bank accounts. This was explained by claiming that the loan-created money was not real money, it was 'credit money' – as against notes and coins that were 'real' money. Like 'fractional reserve banking', 'credit money' was a concept that appeared to explain away the anomaly that banks were creating the public currency through their lending. It is only very recently that it has been recognised by the major monetary authorities that banks are creating new public currency when they lend. Only since 2012 have the International Monetary Fund, the US Federal Reserve and the Bank of England admitted that this is the case.

What is important in banks creating loans in the public currency is that the supply of the public currency is not being determined by the state or the central bank, but by the many private decisions to take out loans. The sovereign power to create money in capitalist economies with extensive banking systems has effectively been privatised. This is enhanced by the neoliberal 'handbag economics' approach to state spending and borrowing. If states are not to 'print money', the only other source of new money must be bank lending. Basing the public currency supply on privately generated debt has many implications.

The main problem is that access to banks is dependent upon financial status, and access to loans even more so. A bank-generated supply of money must gravitate towards the better-off members of society. As was the experience of the eighteenth century, loans are most easily raised by the already-wealthy. The more commercially oriented the banking system, the more it will be driven by profit maximisation, lending to the well-heeled and to the most successful entrepreneurs. The poorer the citizens, the smaller the business, the less likely they will be able to access affordable loans, or any loans at all.

There may also be ecological consequences. The need to repay loans with interest requires constant expansion. This will not necessarily cause immediate ecological exploitation and damage, but it will drive production and consumption. There will be less incentive to slow down, reduce waste and engage in less consumerism.

Finally there is the problem of debt itself. If people, businesses and governments can take no more debt, the supply of the public currency will dry up. This was the fear of governments when the 2007–08 financial crisis struck, as will be discussed in the next chapter.

FIVE

The sorcerer's apprentice: magic money out of control

The 'Sorcerer's Apprentice' is a poem written by the German writer Goethe in 1797. The sorcerer asks the apprentice to fetch water. Being lazy, the apprentice waits until the sorcerer leaves and then steals one of the magic spells to get a broom to fetch the water. This seems to work well and soon there is sufficient water. Unfortunately the apprentice does not know the magic spell to make the broom stop. More and more water is brought until the place is flooded. The apprentice breaks the broom in half, but this just means it brings twice as much. Eventually the sorcerer returns, stops the mayhem and tells the apprentice to leave the spells to wiser heads.

Kate Mc

This is an apt analogy for the financial crisis of 2007–08, the subject of this chapter. The apprentice is the banking sector. The magic spell is the capacity of the banks to create money through debt. A major recipient was the financial sector, which used 'leverage' – that is, debt – to fuel its activities. The regulatory discipline that had been in place since the Great Depression had been breaking down since the 1970s. By 2007–08 banks and other financial agencies were on an orgy of debt-funded speculative activity that was more akin to gambling than traditional financial investment. Debt itself in the form of mortgages became a key focus for investment. Aggressive selling of mortgages to poor people eventually proved to be the weak point in the speculative dam. The chapter opens with one of the first signs of crisis, the failure of a small bank in the North-East of England (Box 5.1). I then go on to explain why the 'leveraged' activities of the financial sector were so precarious. Finally, I describe how the sorcerers, states and monetary authorities had to step back in to rescue the situation.

Box 5.1: Bank on the rocks

On 14 September 2007 a queue of people were lining up outside a small northern bank in the UK. They wanted their money back. The trigger for the run on the Northern Rock bank was a media report that it had needed to go to the Bank of England for a loan. It was the first bank run in Britain since 1866. The run began on a Friday. Throughout the weekend the chief executive of the bank tried to convince the crowds that the bank was fundamentally sound. The Governor of the Bank of England also tried to calm the panic. Nevertheless, the run continued, with Northern Rock paying out around a billion pounds a day.

By Monday 17 September the queues continued to grow and there were rumbles about the viability of other banks and building societies. The run was stopped that day by an unprecedented statement by the Chancellor of the Exchequer, the government minister in charge of the state Treasury. He declared that the government gave its full backing to all Northern Rock savers and would guarantee all deposits currently in place. In February 2008 the bank was nationalised. It eventually returned to the private sector in 2011.

A run is what a bank dreads because, as we have seen, banks do not have money in the way the fairy tale (see Box 1.1) would imply. There are no vaults full of gold or huge piles of banknotes. Instead, most money held in banks takes the form of a record of numbers, many of which are created by the banks themselves when they make loans. What is special about that money is that it is declared to be a record of bank accounts created as public currency. Bank accounts are not records of the bank's money (Barclays' guineas, Santander's florins), they are numbers of pounds, dollars or euros. The money held in bank accounts is treated as being as valid as banknotes or coin. Coin, paper money, plastic card or electronic transfer are all money because they all have the status of the public currency. All are accepted as a means of transferring value. People readily accept payment through the transfer of money numbers on the assumption that they can hand them on in payment themselves. There is no store of 'real' money that those tokens or records represent, there is only the trust people have in them. That trust in Northern Rock had disappeared.

Northern Rock – a salutary story

The Northern Rock bank started out in 1965 as a building society formed out of two older societies that had been established in the mid-nineteenth century. As a building society its activities were limited to taking in savings and providing mortgages for house buyers. Building societies are part of the social economy, they are neither private nor public. Constitutionally, they are owned and controlled by their members – that is, their account holders. Major decisions are taken at meetings of the owner-members, but in practice most account holders don't get involved in the governance of the society. As a result, decision-making is largely left in the hands of managers. Like many other building societies, Northern Rock felt constrained by the rules under which it had to operate.

In the spirit of the post-'Big Bang' financial deregulation of the mid-1980s, the Northern Rock management wanted to take advantage of the seeming opportunities in the new financial climate. In the US and the UK, Big Bang had seen a bonfire of financial regulation for both high street banks and finance generally. Most of the regulations had arisen from the widespread speculation and bank defaults experienced in the Great Depression of the 1930s. Major features of post-Depression bank regulation were the strict separation of financial activities such as banking, investment and insurance, and the control of bank lending.

Under Big Bang the regulatory authorities loosened these controls. Financial firms and banks could combine their activities, leading to a wave of takeovers and amalgamations. Lending became more speculative. Investment banks, in which savings were at risk with no back-up from the central bank, linked up with high street deposit-taking banks, whose activities were licensed and supported by the state monetary authorities. Given the way that licensed banks could create new money through loans, the whole financial sector became plugged in to a banking money-creation machine that fuelled a totally unregulated world of lending and borrowing between high street banks, investment banks, financial companies and speculators.

As a building society, Northern Rock was still subject to restrictive rules to safeguard the savings of its members. It could access the promised land of Big Bang only if it became a private sector bank – that is, if it left the social economy sector for the private sector. This would involve converting the member-owners into shareholders. This was done by giving all account holders a certain number of shares in the privatised bank. Such a move was hotly contested by social-economy activists, but a combination of very low membership participation in the governance of the societies, and the attraction of receiving several hundred pounds through selling their shares, led most members to vote yes in a postal ballot.

One unsavoury aspect of this period was 'carpetbaggers', who saw that building societies were issuing shares to all account holders equally, no matter how long they had held an account or how much money they had saved above a minimum amount. Carpetbaggers opened savings accounts in several building societies and then agitated for them to convert into private banks so that they could benefit from the windfall of new shares. Northern Rock Building Society converted into a bank in 1997.

As a building society, Northern Rock had been a major contributor to local charitable causes. In recognition of a concern that Northern Rock as a bank would lose its social ethos when it converted to a bank in 1997, 15% of the share capital was put into a charitable arm, the Northern Rock Foundation, which also received 5% of Northern Rock's pre-tax profits each year. The Foundation became a very important donor organisation in the local area, funding a wide range of social, sporting and cultural activities in the region. It was one of the most charitable companies in the FTSE 100. A few years after the bank was re-privatised the Foundation ceased to exist.

Despite its regional focus and relatively small number of branches as compared with national banks and building societies, Northern Rock became a leader in the UK mortgage field, particularly for first-time buyers. In the first six months of 2007 it had increased its share of the mortgage market by over 50% and was issuing one in five of all UK mortgages. It was also helping to enhance home-ownership by offering not only mortgages that covered 100% of the value of the house; a quarter of its loans were 125% 'Together' mortgages. As the name implies, these mortgages lent 25% more than the value of the house. The loans were popular as they provided extra funding for the costs associated with a house move. At the time of its collapse Northern Rock had around six thousand employees, many thousands of members, deposits of £24 billion and a loan book of £100 billion.

As a relatively small bank, but a major lender, Northern Rock was at a disadvantage in the interbank clearing process. If there were only one bank, the money-creation process would be unproblematic. Money created as a loan would merely move between the account of the borrower (someone buying a house) and the account of the recipient (the person selling the house). No money would actually leave the bank. However, there is more than one bank. Money does leave the lending bank if the recipient of the loan has an account at another bank.

Because of its small number of branches and relatively low level of deposits as against the large number of borrowers, Northern Rock found less people transferring money in from other banks than it had borrowers transferring money out. True, over time the borrowers would transfer all the money back in as they repaid their loans, but this was not fast enough to cover the immediate amount of money Northern Rock needed to settle its imbalance with other banks.

There were two ways Northern Rock could deal with the imbalance. It could sell on the loans to bring in new money or use the loans as security to borrow money to cover the gap. Those buying up Northern Rock loans needed to be assured that the loans were safe, that borrowers would not default. Those lending Northern Rock money needed to be assured not only that the loans it had made were good security, but that Northern Rock was solvent, that it would stay in business long enough to repay the debt. As long as Northern Rock could attract investors to buy its loans, and the income from the remaining mortgage loans was greater than the cost of its own borrowing, the bank was viable.

However, unlike mortgages, which are repaid over many years, the loans that Northern Rock was using to fund them were short term. This was not a problem if new loans could be taken out to pay off the previous loans coming due. The problem came when the financial sector seized up as the 2007–08 crisis began to grip. Northern Rock could not raise any new loans from other banks to cover its previous loans. Also, the bottom had dropped out of the market in selling customers' loans, following mortgage defaults in the US. This is why Northern Rock had to go to the Bank of England for an emergency loan.

Under UK banking regulations there was a deposit guarantee scheme that secured deposits up to £35,000. However, this was not sufficient to stop the run on the bank. To prevent any contagion spreading across the banking sector, the UK Treasury guaranteed all Northern Rock deposits. The bank was also given a loan of £8 billion. Despite a huge collapse in its market value and share price, Northern Rock was fundamentally sound. By September 2008 it had repaid half of its government loans. Its loan book was viable and there was relatively little bad debt. In 2010 a new Conservative–Liberal Democrat coalition government was voted in with a pro-privatisation agenda, and in 2011 Northern Rock was sold for around a fifth of its pre-collapse value.

Smoke and mirrors: shadow banking

The model of banking adopted by Northern Rock to fund its mortgage lending became known as shadow banking as it involved activities that were not visible to traditional methods of scrutiny. The main instrument for scrutiny of banks and businesses is the balance sheet, which records assets and liabilities. Because Northern Rock was selling on its mortgages or using them as security for loans, these did not appear in its balance sheet. Thus it did not become clear how dependent the bank was becoming on its ability to raise loans from other banks or to find purchasers to buy up customer loans.

The main mechanism of shadow banking was securitisation. Mortgage lending and other loans were turned into financial investments. Loans were put together in bundles of mortgage-backed securities or Collateralised Debt Obligations and sold outright or as a repo (repurchase agreement). A repo is when something is sold for an agreed amount with a commitment by the seller to buy the investment back at a later date at a higher price. A repo is to all intents and purposes a loan, with the 'sold' item being held as security and the higher price that is paid to buy it back covering the interest.

The bundles of mortgages and other types of loan (car loans, consumer credit) were not sold exclusively to one buyer. They were 'diced and sliced' to create investments of different interest rates and prices, reflecting different levels of risk. Those charging the least interest for a repo, or paying the most for their share of the securitised bundle, would be the first to be paid out if some of the loans defaulted. Those receiving a higher interest rate or paying less would be the next in line and so on. As a further security, insurance was arranged through Credit Default Swaps, where holders of the bundles of loans would pay a fee to insure against the debts defaulting. Banks and financial businesses were locked in to a network of securitisation as sellers, lenders, buyers and insurers, often combining some or all of these activities.

Levitation: floating on a cloud of debt

As well as buying and selling the debt of bank customers, the financial sector became a major borrower itself. Investors' money was enhanced by 'leverage' – borrowed money used to increase the value of a particular speculation. Large amounts of debt could pivot on quite a small initial investment, like the magicians' trick of producing a bunch of flowers from a flat sleeve, or an endless stream of flags from a small container. In the same way as pressure on a small lever can move a large boulder, debt piled on a small amount of initial investment can vastly increase the profit made.

The principle is simple. If £100 were invested in a stock market or currency gamble which would bring a return of 10%, that would bring a total return of £110. However, if a short-term loan of £1,000 at a cost of 5% were added to that investment or currency gamble, the return would increase by an additional 10% of that £1,000 (£100), less 5% interest charge (£50). The original sum of £100 would then have made £160, a much better return. Everyone would seem to win. The original investor has a high return; the short-term money lender has a fee and interest. The intermediating fund manager takes a fee. All is well – unless the investment fails.

Another way of enhancing speculative investments is to buy 'on the margin'. This involves agreeing to buy a share or some currency at a particular value but paying only a small deposit rather than the full amount up front. Again, as long as the investment is worth more than you have agreed to pay, a healthy profit can be made on a small outlay.

In the build-up to the financial crisis most investment banks and other investment funds relied on leverage (borrowing) to enhance profits. Private equity and hedge funds, in particular, found banks willing to lend incredibly cheaply to speculative finance companies. Private equity companies specialise in 'leveraged buyouts'. They borrowed money to buy out the shares or the ownership of other companies, with the aim of re-selling the shares or ownership at a profit in the future.

Hedge funds gamble on anything – shares, securities, futures, currencies – often using short-term borrowing to make the trade. This is a long way from the original meaning of hedging against adverse circumstances, such as a poor harvest or a drop in prices. The real growth in speculative hedge funds stemmed from the 1970s, when currency exchange rates were floated. This followed the ending of the 1944 arrangement made at Bretton Woods in New Hampshire, US for countries to fix their exchange rates in relation to the dollar.

The activities of hedge funds can have a major impact in world currency markets. It has been estimated that speculation could account for up to 95% of daily international currency movements. The speculative 'bet' may be made through trading in a particular asset such as a share or a currency, or bets can be placed on how particular investments will move. The latter is the difference between betting on a particular horse in a race and betting on how far in front of the next horse the winner will be. These latter are known as derivatives. With their ability to predict future events, hedge funds seemed to have the secret of magical money making, with its opaque science of algorithmic trading based on computer programs developed by so-called 'rocket scientists'. The failure of one of these ventures revealed the central role of bank lending in supporting speculative activities.

Box 5.2: The 'too-big-to-fail' hedge fund

In 1994 a hedge fund, Long Term Capital Management (LTCM), was set up to exploit what was thought to be a fail-safe method of speculation developed by its Economics 'Nobel' prize-winning partners, Robert Merton and Myron S. Scholes. For its first few years, LTCM was hugely successful, building its capital to $5 billion. However, in 1998 it faced huge potential losses because of something the model was supposed to anticipate: the unexpected. The Russian state had defaulted on its debt repayments.

LTCM had adopted the highly leveraged hedge fund formula of borrowing extensively to expand its speculative activity with credit facilities at more than fifty banks. Its main activity was derivative betting 'on the margin', making a large bet with a small initial outlay. Estimates of its leverage (borrowing in relation to actual investments) ranged from 35:1 to 100:1. According to the head of the Federal Reserve at the time, Alan Greenspan, LTCM borrowed around $120 billion and had derivative positions worth around $1.25 trillion.[1]

> As the biggest hedge fund at that time, if LTCM had had to unwind all its 'bets', the impact on the financial markets would have been enormous. It was deemed too big to fail, and sixteen of the world's biggest banks were called in by the US central bank, the Federal Reserve, to put up rescue money of $3.6 billion to enable LTCM to unwind its positions slowly. The case was made to the banks that they would lose much more money if LTCM collapsed.

As head of the Federal Reserve, Greenspan was proud that no Treasury money was involved in the LTCM debacle. He obviously did not count the massive write-off and rescues made by the banks as disbursing public money. Although LTCM's crisis was in 1998, lessons seem not to have been learned before the crisis of 2007–08.

Hedge funds are an emblem of a globalised casino economy based on debt, with most of their funds held offshore to avoid tax. They have had a huge impact on stock markets, currencies and other areas of financial speculation. At its peak, the global derivative market was more than ten times the size of world output of goods and services. Given their need for high levels of bank loans, hedge funds were early casualties of the credit crunch. By 2009 many funds in Europe and the US were either closed or running down their activities. However, this caution towards speculative investment was short lived. By 2010 the *Wall Street Journal* was reporting that bank lending to hedge funds and private equity firms was back at the same levels as before the crisis.[2]

While debt was growing apace for speculators, other forms of debt were also growing. Part of the bonfire of regulation was the ending of restrictions on various forms of personal and household credit. Borrowing became a way of life, with household debt in 2006 at nearly 122% of Gross Domestic Product (GDP) in the US and a similar figure in the UK. It was household debt linked to financial speculation that threatened the Western banking system in 2007–08.

Poor people dry up the magic money machine (temporarily)

Following the collapse of the dotcom boom at the end of the twentieth century, money, particularly in the US, was very cheap to borrow, but opportunities for profitable investment were limited. Debt became pivotal to the next financial boom. Not only did debt enhance speculative activities, but debt itself became a commodity to be traded in, and gambled on. Mortgage lending in particular became an increasingly important source of income for the banks. This was a new area of lending for banks, as traditionally mortgages were generally issued through specialist agencies.

Before the 1990s nearly two-thirds of British mortgages were provided by building societies. With the privatisation of building societies and the new mechanisms of raising loan finance, this had slumped to one fifth, with high street banks taking the lion's share. In the US mortgages had traditionally been set at a fixed interest rate and were mainly underwritten by two large organisations: Fannie Mae (Federal National Mortgage Agency) and Freddie Mac (Federal Home Mortgage Corporation). Between them they provided backing for half the nation's mortgages, worth around $5 trillion. This made home-ownership manageable, as borrowers knew that their mortgage repayments would remain the same throughout the period of their loan. British building societies also had predictable interest rates.

What changed in the US was the introduction of variable rate mortgages. By 2007 nearly 50% of US mortgages were issued as variable rate. This made them financially exciting for lenders, as instead of all borrowers being treated the same, with predictable levels of repayment, borrowers could find themselves facing higher repayments if interest rates rose. New mortgage companies were sprouting up, knowing that they could easily sell on any mortgages they could persuade people to take. There was a chain of investors ready to buy up the mortgages, or to lend more money to facilitate new housing loans, as, traditionally, mortgages had been a rock-solid investment with very few defaults.

With banks and mortgage companies eager to lend, money flooded into the housing market. House prices began to rise dramatically and people started to think of a home not as somewhere to live but as a financial asset. Longer-term home-owners found themselves with homes worth much more than their existing mortgage commitments. This was another great opportunity for mortgage lenders as people began to 'release' that value by taking out another mortgage.

The undoing of this lucrative lending spree was the spread of lending to more economically vulnerable people. The main attraction for lenders was that low-income house-owners could be charged a higher level of interest because they were deemed to be a greater risk.

Dubious methods were used to pressure people into taking out mortgages, mainly in the form of deals that seemed very good but lasted only a short time. Unscrupulous mortgage agents persuaded people that they could easily afford the repayments because they quoted 'teaser' rates of interest. What the new home-owner didn't realise was that the interest rate would rise dramatically after a few weeks or months. For US house-owners used to a fixed rate mortgage for the lifetime of the loan, it was natural to assume that the original rate of payment would continue. The personal circumstances of the borrower were also ignored. Information given when taking out a mortgage was not verified, including ability to pay. This led to the notorious NINJA loans – no income, no job, no questions asked.

The reason for such a casual approach was that those issuing the mortgage intended to sell on the debt very quickly. This meant there was little incentive to minimise risk. Risk assessment for traditional mortgage lending was through careful scrutiny of the borrower. In the new climate, credit-worthiness was not assessed at the level of the individual mortgage borrower; instead, it was carried out through statistical calculations and profiling. Measures were used such as age, location or type of property. All seemed well. More people could now afford houses, or were able to raise money from their existing house. Mortgage companies could take their fee and sell on their loans. Banks could take their fee and sell on the securitised mortgage to investors who were hungry for higher returns. Insurance companies guaranteed against default.

The problems in the sub-prime mortgage market emerged as the boom in US house prices started to slow from 2004 onwards and interest rates rose. Defaults on mortgages within the first three months were virtually unheard of, but they were beginning to happen. Poorer families were starting to lose their homes and mortgage companies were going out of business. Those who had invested by buying up the bundles of mortgage loans began to question their value.

When they were first launched the innovative mortgage-backed securities had been given a top investment rating of AAA. These were set by rating agencies, respected financial advisors that make a judgement as to how free from risk an investment is likely to be. An AAA rating allowed more conservative organisations to invest, such as pension funds. The AAA rating for investment in mortgage loans reflected the fact that mortgage defaults were more or less unknown in the US. Now, when defaults were happening, investors did not know what their bundles of mortgages were worth.

The sub-prime crisis was also a crisis for the banks. They had made loans that would now have to sit on their balance sheets because they could not sell them, and many of those loans could be defaulting. The whole securitised system had been a merry-go-round of buying and selling debts and risks. Regulated and non-bank financial institutions were at one and the same time buyers and sellers of securities and guarantors of risk. Rather than sharing risk through these complex networks of investments, the securitisation process spread risk. This impacted on the vital job of clearing payments between banks and offering short-term credit to each other to balance the books. The fear of mortgage default began to raise questions about other types of financial investment and the whole structure of 'shadow banking' shuddered to a halt. Northern Rock was an early casualty of this 'credit crunch'. Banks, saddled with unknown levels of risk, refused to offer any more credit in any direction (Box 5.3).

Box 5.3: The 'not-too-big-to-fail' investment bank

September 2008 was another critical turning point, when the more than 150-year-old US investment bank Lehman Brothers, with 25,000 employees, was allowed to fail. Lehman had been heavily involved in the new financial investments and in 2007 was thought to have borrowed around $30 for every $1 invested. Unable to find any new investors or lenders to help bridge the billions of dollars shortfall in its finances, Lehman appealed to the US Federal Reserve for support. This was refused, as Lehman was not a high street 'retail' bank, it was only an investment bank, and should not be bailed out. Lehman collapsed, and nearly took the entire Western banking system down with it.

Why did the failure of an investment bank in the US cause such a crisis? Investment banks were not the same as high street banks. They did not take deposits or make loans, they took in investments that people knew were potentially at risk. The problem lay in the way high street banks had themselves become involved in investment lending. If Lehman could not pay back its loans this would threaten the solvency of the banks that had made those loans. The danger was that this would trigger a run on the high street banks.

The most pressing fear that triggered state action was the lack of cash in the system. If people tried to withdraw cash in large numbers automated teller machines (ATMs) would dry up in a very short time. This would expose the truth about modern money. It did not exist. Money was not the solid coinage of the fairy tale. It was a delicate structure of debts and promises. It would become awfully clear that the monetary emperor had no clothes. This was not just a crisis of finance, it was a crisis of money. Public trust in the monetary system would dry up with the ATMs.

The sorcerer returns: saving the banks

As the crisis gripped, the shares of private sector banks collapsed because fears were widespread that the loans they had made had gone 'toxic' and were unlikely to be repaid. As the North Atlantic and European banking and financial sectors were so interconnected there was no 'firewall' to stop the contagion. Unlike in the US in 1907, where one banker, J.P. Morgan, was strong enough to stop the panic, there were no untainted banks. The only grown-ups left in the room were states. What they did was dramatically expand their spending to rescue their banks. They did not obtain this money from taxes. This would be impossible anyway, because tax income was drying up as economies contracted in the face of the financial collapse. They could not borrow the money because the reason states had to step in was that lending in the banking and financial sector had ground to a halt.

What the states did was to 'print money'. This was not literal; states did not set up round-the-clock printing presses to create banknotes. Nor did they raid their central banks for gold or some other form of 'real' money to 'back' their expenditure. Modern money, as we have seen, exists mainly in the form of bank accounts, so states credited the bank accounts of various organisations with additional numbers, or gave guarantees that bank accounts would be honoured. This dramatically expanded the budgets of states so that their 'deficit' increased – that is, the level of state spending as against state income.

The main beneficiaries of state largesse were the banks. Funds were channelled to banks to enable them to continue operating. If this was not sufficient, states took over their running. As well as nationalising Northern Rock, the British government invested £20 billion in Royal Bank of Scotland (RBS), one of the world's largest banks, taking more than 80% of its ownership. The parlous position of RBS was so extreme that ten years later the bulk of the bank still remained in public ownership.

RBS illustrates how far out of control the sorcerer's apprentice banks were. In 2008 RBS had made a loss of more than £24 billion, much of this loss resulting from its disastrous multi-billion pound takeover of the Dutch bank ABN Amro. This deal went ahead despite the fact that Northern Rock had already collapsed. What the crisis also revealed were the huge salaries and other payments in the financial and banking sector. There was public revulsion at the fact that the boss of RBS at the time of the crisis had voluntarily left the bank with a full pension of over £700,000 a year. Under intense pressure, he later offered to give up part of the pension. He was also stripped of a knighthood that gave him the title of 'Sir'.

Governments also set up funds to buy or insure toxic debts. RBS put £325 billion into the UK government's toxic debt insurance scheme. Another amalgamated bank, Lloyds/HBoS, put in £260 billion of potentially bad loans which it had made. A similar TARP (Troubled Assets Relief Program) in the US had spent $700 billion by the end of 2010 buying up bad loans from its banks. The US also directly supported its banks. The government took a large stake in Citigroup, a huge multinational banking and financial services company, as well as providing new money to support the solvency of several other banks. At times, the US and UK governments were putting more money into the banks than their value as businesses.

Some surprising differences emerged. The Spanish bank Santander largely weathered the storm because of tight Spanish banking law, whereas in Switzerland, well known for its banking prowess, the Swiss banking giant UBS faced huge losses and needed state support. Even the staid German banks did not escape. The German government had to make substantial provision for toxic debt, and took a stake in its second-largest bank, Commerzbank. Even Deutsche Bank made a loss of nearly €4 billion in 2008, its first loss in fifty years. However, state-owned banks fared little better. The German state-owned regional bank Bayern Landesbanken suffered substantial losses. Nor did building societies escape. In Britain several had to be taken over or merged with stronger organisations.

In the first year of the crisis the total amount spent in bank bailouts had cost the UK government at least £600 billion. This represented more than the whole annual UK budget in the year before the crisis began. Estimates of the total cost of the 2007–08 crisis to the state and monetary authorities in the US alone range from $13 trillion to more than $20 trillion by 2012–13.

One reason for the huge cost of the bailouts was the rapid growth of the banking and financial sectors in relation to GDP. GDP measures the sum total of goods and services currently produced in an economy. It does not count bank balances or rises in asset values, such as the price of houses. As a result of the financial expansion the total amount of money accumulated in bank accounts was much bigger than the GDP in many countries. At its peak, RBS with its £1.8 trillion balance sheet was larger than the total UK GDP, The total of all the UK banks' balance sheets could be as high as £5 trillion. The Irish state, faced with the same dilemma, guaranteed all of its banks' deposits – a commitment worth double its GDP.

What is remarkable is that very few bankers were punished for their actions in the run-up to the crisis and very little changed in banking and financial practice. An exception was Iceland, where banks were allowed to go bust and several bankers were given jail terms for financial misdemeanours.

During late 2008, and certainly by the beginning of 2009, it was clear that putting money into the banks was not enough. Money was needed in the economy as a whole. Governments around the world dropped all pretensions of the independence of markets and started to pump money into their financial sectors and the wider economy. This was done through a combination of government spending, ultra-low interest rates and the obscurely named 'quantitative easing'. This is a euphemism for the state again exercising its power to create money through its central bank and put it directly into the economy. This can be done in a number of ways.

The central bank can buy loans made by investors or banks to businesses, in the hope that they will invest the money in a new venture. The government can also buy its own debt back, again giving money to the holder to hopefully invest productively. The central bank can also release money directly to the state treasury for public spending, although this is generally administered as a loan. In the US a programme of buying government debt and other forms of debt with new electronic money reached nearly $4 trillion by 2015. In the UK £475 billion was spent buying back government debt. Although new public money was spent buying back public sector debt, those debts were not cancelled. They remained on the books and the Conservative–Liberal Democrat government used them, together with the public expenditure deficit created by the crisis, to justify a harsh austerity programme.

The European Central Bank (ECB) was more resistant to the idea of active monetary intervention, as it did not fit with its neoliberal rules about lending to governments or issuing money directly. According to its rules, the ECB cannot directly buy or administer sovereign debt. It can create new money, but only in response to demand from the commercial banks. However, facing the possibility of a collapse in European economies in 2015, it began a programme of quantitative easing.

The danger in quantitative easing through the financial sector is that the money will just go to the same people who have contributed to the financial collapse in the first place. Direct public spending on infrastructure or services, lending to productive companies or relieving the financial pressure on households could produce much more immediate help for people. There are many constructive ways in which new money can be issued and these will be discussed the final chapter.

Despite all the efforts by states to rescue their economies from debt-fuelled booms, success is not inevitable. Japan has tried a range of measures since its crash in the early 1990s following a huge boom in property values. It has had interest rates near zero since 2001. Money was poured into the banks. Increases in government spending and quantitative easing have been tried without notable success. Japan has tried cash payments to all households, loans for people between jobs, tax cuts for home-owners, support for banks and credits for small businesses, all to little avail. However, Japan remains a major economy, and shows that a country can still be near the top of the league despite a seemingly large national debt.

By the middle of 2009 the world economy was still looking at decline, with unemployment rising. Public spending was coming under pressure following the huge outlays on support for the financial sector, which had driven up public sector deficits. Rather than focus on the failure of the banks and financial sector, neoliberalism took its chance to attack its main target: the welfare state.

Bad magic: austerity

The initial widespread public response to the crisis made it seem as if the reign of the financial markets and handbag economics must come to an end. The financial sector was in disgrace and the centrality of public finance to its survival was plain to see. However, the window of opportunity for change was lost. Social and political movements that might have been in a position to present an alternative monetary and financial strategy had none. Certainly there were spirited protest movements, such as Occupy and the 1% campaign, but no proposals were put forward that could challenge conventional thinking. In the absence of a clear political and intellectual alternative, the bank bailouts were turned against the public sector. Rather than the banking crisis, and the misbehaviour of the banks, being seen as the problem, the pressure was turned against what was seen as unpayable sovereign debt. The answer then became to reduce public expenditure through austerity measures until the debt returned to 'acceptable' levels.

The 2007–08 crisis saw both public debts and deficits increase as the costs of bank rescue and rising welfare expenditure were accompanied by a collapse in tax receipts as the recession bit. The collapse in the British economy meant that the deficit, the gap between government income and expenditure, jumped from 2% to 10%. As conventional economics does not acknowledge that states can create money, any gap in state income is seen as adding to the national debt – that is, a debt deemed to be owed to the financial sector. As a result, UK national debt jumped from 40% of GDP to 80% of GDP.

In Britain at the time of the crisis there was a Labour government in power which followed the Keynesian model of plugging the gap in national spending through public spending, pending the recovery of the market. When the Conservative–Liberal Democrat coalition took power in 2010 it revoked the Keynesian strategy. Rather than seeing the problem as stemming from the financial sector, the neoliberal government took the opportunity to blame the state rather than the market. It launched a programme of austerity to reduce government spending and bring down the national debt.

This handbag economics approach to state spending was bolstered by EU rules limiting states to 60% of GDP for state borrowing and 3% of GDP for state deficits. This was supported by an academic paper that seemed to prove that government debt above 90% of GDP led to a fall in growth.[3] Although the statistical evidence underpinning this finding was later found to be faulty, the damage had been done, and widespread austerity programmes were implemented.[4]

In Britain the stated aim of the austerity programme was to get everyone into work, even if the jobs were low paid and precarious. Cuts were imposed across the board, including expenditure on universal public services, welfare, pensions, public infrastructure. Despite a cut in taxes and slashing public budgets, the deficit and public borrowing remained stubbornly high.

As I will explain more fully in Chapter Seven, the hysteria about government deficits is due to a flawed understanding of how the monetary system works. Deficits should not automatically be seen as a problem. On the contrary, a deficit may be necessary if the debt-based supply of the public currency begins to dry up. The sovereign power that the state retains is the ability to create new currency free of debt. The money created by the central banks to rescue the banks and reboot the economy was not borrowed from anyone. Like banks generally, the central bank can create money just by putting numbers into accounts. However, unlike ordinary banks, the central bank money does not have to be loaned into circulation: it can be directly spent. This is because the power of the central banks to create new money is not a banking power – the power to make loans. Central banks are exercising the sovereign power to create money.

The sovereign power to create money enables seigniorage – that is, benefit of the first use of that money. Where the people are sovereign, the sovereign power to create money can be used to directly benefit the people. There is no need to be beholden to high finance or the market. The ideological justification for privatised control of the creation and circulation of money as debt is that it puts economic responsibility onto the borrower. It is assumed that people, companies and governments would not borrow what they could not repay, nor would lenders lend to those whose credit-worthiness was in doubt. In contrast, states are seen as profligate and inefficient, wasting the taxpayer's money.

The battle then becomes whether the public money supply is a private or a public matter. This confusion comes because, as discussed in the previous chapter, money created privately by banks' lending became synonymous with the public currency. The crisis showed that in the last resort it is the public sorcerer that has to pick up the pieces. In using bank loans extensively for speculative ends, an unsustainable financial order was gambling with public money. The lack of any fundamental challenge to the dominant neoliberal paradigm means that in modern, bank-led money systems the public is taking responsibility for the integrity of its public currency, while the private sector retains control and reaps the financial benefit.

The immense level of the state's resources, including its power to create money – made available in the bank bailout – and the central role of the state in securing money systems, has not led to recognition of the crucial role of the state as a monetary agent. It has not been realised how dependent the financial sector and the privatised money supply system is on explicit and implicit public guarantees. This creates what economists describe as 'moral hazard', whereby financial actors take excessive risk, knowing that the sorcerer inevitably has to bail out the water of the apprentice's mismanagement. While the public have lost control of the bank-created supply of their public currency, they have not shed their liability for it. The state does not have to abdicate in the face of demands from the banks for autonomy in the creation of public money, but to do so it must escape from the hypnotic trance of monetary fairy tales.

The dominance of bank debt means that the public money supply has effectively been privatised. If the public is to regain control over its money supply it needs to reverse the privatisation of the power to create money. The money supply needs to be democratised. I will look at ways that this might be achieved in the final chapter. Before that I will look at attempts to develop money systems without the state sorcerer.

SIX

Ditching the sorcerer:
money without the state

The previous chapter explored what happened when state control of the money system was removed. The bonfire of regulations in the US and the UK in the 1980s let loose a huge wave of money creation through bank lending. Financial markets were liberated and hot money flowed freely across the globe. It seemed as if the era of the sorcerer–state was over. Markets could look after themselves. Unfortunately, within only a few years the system was in crisis and states had to step in once more.

This chapter looks at three approaches to building a monetary system *without* the supervisory role of the state. The first is the euro, which was set up as a transnational currency where control of the money system was seen as a largely administrative exercise informed by a framework of basic rules. The second aims to build a money system without any monetary institutions, whether banks, central banks or states, through the use of cryptocurrencies. This approach sees the generation and circulation of money as a purely technical operation that doesn't need supervision of any sort.

The third approach has a long history. It challenges national currencies and the role of the state by seeking to build monetary communities from the bottom up. There have been many examples of the local creation of currencies, variously described as social, complementary, or parallel to national currencies. These are almost the mirror opposites of the euro and cryptocurrencies, as they emphasise the social function of money rather than seeing it as a neutral technical or administrative matter.

As I have argued that money is both a social and a political phenomenon, it would logically follow that all three approaches are doomed to failure. In the case of the euro and cryptocurrencies, this is because they do not address the problematics of the social and political context of money. Social money, on the other hand, tends to find difficulty confronting the wider political and economic arena.

The euro: a magic potion for peace

As I have mentioned several times, the euro is in many ways the embodiment of modern money. It is clearly and unambiguously fiat money. It makes no pretence to be other than a numerical unit of measurement, comparison and transfer of the face-value of the money. Euro banknotes simply state their numerical value: five, ten, twenty euros. Unlike the British pound, the euro makes no claim to be representing some superior or more valuable form of money. It is not a 'promise to pay' in gold or anything else. Nor does it feel the need to declare itself to be authorised money like the US dollar, which states that it is to be honoured as 'legal tender'. The money system is so much part of people's lives that there is no question that the recognised public currency is valid for all purposes across the Eurozone, whether it exists as banknotes and coin, numbers in a bank account or other monetary record. While the euro is a straightforward and unpretentious *form* of money, it is by no means straightforward in its origins or operation.

While the idea of a euro had been discussed for more than thirty years, it was only formally created in 1999 and was phased in to fully replace existing national currencies by 2002. Although it was hoped that eventually all members of the EU would adopt the euro, only eleven of the then fifteen EU countries joined in the first instance, led by Germany, France and Italy. The most notable member not to join was the UK. By 2018 what had become known as the Eurozone embraced nineteen of the twenty-eight members of the EU, and the UK was not only outside of the euro but was in the throes of disengaging from the EU completely, following the Brexit referendum in 2016.

To understand the euro it is necessary to understand the social and political conditions that lay behind it.

The euro was the culmination of a process set in motion by the desire to avoid further conflict on a continent that had seen two catastrophic wars within thirty years. The overall aim of those who promoted the idea of a pan-European structure was to develop forms of cooperation between previously warring countries in the hope of securing a peaceful future. The political conclusion was that the best way to unite countries socially was to unite them economically. The euro was a late child of this vision.

What is now the EU began life in 1950 as the European Coal and Steel Community. The founding countries were Belgium, France, Germany, Italy, Luxembourg and the Netherlands. Over the years, the size and aims of the organisation grew. In 1973 Denmark, Ireland and Britain joined. Greece joined in 1981 and Spain and Portugal in 1986. Austria, Finland and Sweden followed in 1995. The collapse of the Soviet Union led ultimately to ten new countries joining in 2004, with Bulgaria and Romania adding to that number in 2007. Croatia became the twenty-eighth member in 2013. In 2016 Britain was the first to propose leaving, following a referendum.

As it grew, the structure and programme of the European Economic Community, as it became known, expanded. A political framework was established in the form of a European Parliament, with direct elections first held in 1979 based on proportional representation. Each political party put forward a list of candidates for multiple-member constituencies. Candidates were elected according to the proportion of votes for each party. However, the European Parliament was relatively toothless because the actual running of the EU fell to the European Commission (the European civil service) and the Council of Ministers (the European government). Both the Commission and the Council of Ministers were chosen and appointed by the national governments, not the European Parliament.

Common policies were developed, such as on agriculture and regional development. The approach was based on what became known as a 'social market' perspective whereby national governments and the European structures intervened actively in key markets. The social market model saw capitalist markets as essentially flawed, necessitating a strong role for the state and extensive state protection for citizens. Against this background, coordinated economic policy across Europe, including the idea of a common currency, was seen as a symbol of social and political harmony. People who shared a common money and common progressive economic policies, it was thought, would not go to war. From the perspective of the twenty-first century, where sovereign states have torn themselves apart in civil wars, this thinking looks highly optimistic. Other forces were also afoot as neoliberal ideas took hold that undermined the economic interventionism of the social market ethos.

In the 1980s the social market model was abandoned in favour of an open 'free' market based on neoliberal principles. Championed by Britain's Conservative prime minister Margaret Thatcher, the new approach sought to minimise the role of the state and remove all barriers to the activities of the market. In 1986 the Single European Act was signed, creating a single, integrated market across the member states. Free trade was encouraged by the four freedoms: the movement of goods, services, people and money. This made the case for a single currency an economic one rather than a political one. However, the dream of a politically united Europe was not dead. The Maastricht Treaty of 1992 created the European Union. This envisaged greater political cooperation while maintaining the dominance of commercial interests.

It was against this two-pronged background that the euro was born. The euro was seen as supporting free trade by removing the complication of working with different currencies. However, it also represented one of the most symbolic of political gestures: giving up such a significant national emblem as the national currency in order to cement transnational solidarity.

From administrator to sorcerer: how the euro found its magic

My core argument in this book is that there are two sources of new money that could be described as magic money trees: state spending and bank lending. In modern economies central banks are connected to both. As an arm of the state, a central bank can exercise the sovereign power to create money for public use. As the organisation responsible for managing the public currency it also creates money to support the banking sector.

However, according to neoliberal handbag economics, the state's sovereign power to create money must be curtailed. All new money must be generated by the market. In the absence of state-created money, the only source of new public currency would be bank lending. The founding principles governing the ECB in its management of the euro conformed to the neoliberal rubric. The ECB, based in Frankfurt, was only to engage in the provision of new, publicly generated money through lending to the banking sector. Most emphatically, the ECB was not to give or lend money to states.

If states wanted more money than they raised in taxes, they should go to the financial sector for a loan. States did this by issuing interest-bearing bonds that were bought by financial institutions. The bonds were for a fixed period of time, after which they were redeemed by the state. Even then, states were to be restricted on how much money they could raise in this way. Under the Stability and Growth Pact of 1997 member states were instructed to keep public expenditure deficits below 3% of GDP, while total public debt was to be kept below 60% of GDP. It was clear from these restrictions that state deficit or borrowing was not to be a feature of the euro money supply.

The neoliberal remit for the ECB lasted barely ten years. As the crisis of 2007–08 developed, the ECB found itself more and more drawn in to supporting state borrowing. Not only were states in difficulties as their economies collapsed, but the banks and financial institutions that had bought state bonds also faced the possibility that the debts would not be repaid. The bailout was as much for the banks as for the states. States such as Ireland, Portugal and, most notably, Greece found themselves unable to meet their debt repayments and the ECB, together with the EU and the International Monetary Fund, had to provide funds to bail them out.

Trying to stimulate the collapsing money supply through bank lending, the ECB pumped €1 trillion into European banks through cheap loans. However, most of the money was left in their ECB reserve accounts, as banks failed to increase their lending in a hostile economic environment. To try to persuade the banks to lend, the ECB charged them to keep the money in their accounts. By the middle of 2012 Mario Draghi, head of the ECB, was forced to take a more interventionist position. He declared that 'The ECB is ready to do whatever it takes to preserve the euro.' By 2014 he had cut interest rates to almost zero, and by 2015 the ECB undertook 'outright monetary transactions' – that is, quantitative easing – not just providing cheap money to banks but buying up various forms of debt directly, including state debt.

The experience of the Eurozone indicates that the market economy cannot be separated from the public economy. Bank lending alone cannot sustain a public money supply. When the market fails, and the bank-loan money-creating machine grinds to a halt, the sovereign power of money creation is needed, even if it is dressed up as government borrowing. The aim of keeping the euro as a purely administrative system failed. The ECB could not just passively respond to the demands of a market-oriented banking sector. At the minimum it took drastic action to try to get the banks lending again. As the crisis progressed it became more involved in bailouts and radical monetary interventions.

The problem then becomes one of what will be the politics of the changing role of the ECB? When all decisions were to be left to the market via bank borrowing, there appeared to be no need for the ECB to be subject to overt political oversight. However, if the ECB is to be involved in bailouts, state finances and other active interventions, there needs to be a political framework to determine priorities. Which states are to be rescued? Which states or public organisations should receive loans or funds? This would seem to require some form of political structure to determine monetary policy.

The neoliberal mandate for the European monetary system was led by the dominant Eurozone states, particularly Germany. However, the weaker economies of the southern and eastern European states would seem to require a more active interventionist monetary strategy. The neoliberal approach to the weak Eurozone economies following the 2007–08 crisis led to the imposition of austerity on the public sector and the privatisation of public assets. Both strategies were most notably imposed on Greece. I would argue that destroying the public economy doesn't strengthen the market; it weakens it. What is needed is enough direct deficit spending to re-float the private sector, as will be described in the next chapter. New money should be used to build public infrastructure and build up public services until enough money is in circulation to support a vibrant commercial sector.

The neoliberal view of money takes a zero-sum perspective: Greek rescue is seen as a burden on the German taxpayer. This totally misunderstands what money is. There is no shortage of money. In the same way as banks do not raid bank accounts when they make a loan, states do not pick the taxpayer's pocket to pay for public expenditure. German workers did not pay up front for the Greek rescue; it did not come directly out of their wage packet. In fact, they may well benefit from a re-booted Greek economy that increases the purchase of German products. Banks that had lent to the Greek state certainly benefited from the bailout as debts were paid down.

The euro was an attempt to create, through the ECB, supra-national technical support for a privatised transnational public currency supply. This would be circulated through bank lending. What was missing was a politics of money at the European level. While there were stringent transnational economic rules for states, bank lending was not regulated and commercial interest rates were not controlled. The banking and financial sectors in some of the peripheral economies exploded. A key example was Ireland, where the banking system expanded until it was eight times GDP. Spain also saw a housing boom based on borrowed money. However, the euro cannot be entirely blamed for such events, as the UK and the US also saw rapid uncontrolled growth of their financial sectors.

Although in its operation the euro was seen as a purely administrative matter, it was conceived in a social and political context. Like the traditional money of pre-market societies it was envisaged as a means of avoiding conflict. However, unlike in pre-state communities, the euro's symbolism did not emerge from historical custom; it was a conscious politically inspired creation. The irony of the market orientation of the money supply in the Eurozone is that the aim of the European project remains social and political. The assumption is that a people united by a common money would develop a common identity. As many of its critics have pointed out, the logic of the implementation of the euro is that it is part of a wider political project to build a transnational European state. The evidence of this book would also support that logic. Money cannot be purely commercial, it must also be social and public. It remains to be seen how the ECB will address this dilemma.

A seeming solution to both the need for state regulation and the problem of debt-based money appeared in the form of cryptocurrencies.

The magician who disappeared: bitcoin

A recent initiative that aims to eliminate any public or banking framework for money is the creation of a non-state, non-bank digital currency. The first such decentralised and autonomously programmed cryptocurrency, bitcoin, was launched in 2009. It was developed by a person or group called Satoshi Nakamoto, whom no one has yet identified and who has not been heard from since late 2010.

Bitcoin is basically an electronic code, programmed to limit the total number of the coin-codes that can be generated to 21 million. There are two main elements: the creation of new bitcoin codes and the monitoring of transactions. Each 'coin' has a unique number and is located in an electronic 'wallet'. There is no link between the wallet and the holder of that wallet except a key code that lets her access the wallet. Transactions are therefore entirely private. As the electronic coins pass between electronic wallets they are recorded in an open record of transactions. This builds into a large and growing database of all bitcoins in existence and which wallet they are in. It is claimed that this eliminates the possibility of counterfeit or fraud, as all transactions are posted throughout the system.

The program does not run itself. Human actors are needed to create the new bitcoin units ('miners') and to build the monitoring database of transactions. The latter is a 'block-chain' design. This links groups of transactions into chains and then saves them in a block of data that is theoretically unalterable. Each transaction is broadcast through the entire network before being assembled into blocks as a permanent record. No one oversees the system but 'miners' provide the computer power to process transactions. Miners 'bid' to carry out a bunch of transactions, usually ten minutes' worth (around a thousand), by completing a complex mathematical problem. The miner is then chosen at random from all the bidders – miners can make more than one bid. They are paid in bitcoin. As the system gets larger the 'miners' need banks of computers to manage the database.

Taking part in the generation and monitoring of activity in digital currencies requires technical skills and high levels of computer power to drive it. A major drawback is the amount of computer power needed as the number of bitcoins and transactions expands. It has been estimated that recording a bitcoin transaction can take five thousand times more energy than processing a credit card transaction. Together with the energy needed to 'mine' new bitcoins, if all global transactions were done on the bitcoin method it would probably take more power than is generated on the whole planet. It remains to be seen if there is a technological solution to make the block-chain method more sustainable.

The main question for cryptocurrencies is whether they can mount a real challenge to public currencies. Like them, they are fiat money. There is nothing backing cryptocurrencies other than people's willingness to accord them value and/or accept them in payment. At the time of writing there were around 1,500 cryptocurrencies available online with an estimated total value of around $400 billion, of which around a third is bitcoin. It is doubtful that cryptocurrencies could meet the demands of global trade, let alone public expenditure. If all 21 million bitcoins were created and each was worth $50,000 that would total $1 trillion. The current total value of all coins and notes globally could be at least eight times that, and if all the money held in bank accounts were added, the value would be many times more.

When they were first launched, bitcoins were virtually given away. Generating them was relatively easy and thousands could be bought for a small amount of regular currency. Over time they increased in value. While the original aim had been to create a neutral currency to enable trade, bitcoin and similar cryptocurrencies morphed into commodities that were bought as financial investments. Physical versions of the electronic currencies were also being sold as novelties and investments. The year 2017 saw a highly speculative bubble in bitcoin. At the beginning of the year a bitcoin was worth around $900. By the end of 2017 it was almost $18,000. By August 2018 a bitcoin was worth only a third of its peak value. Many central banks saw this as an unsustainable bubble and issued warnings that bitcoin was not suitable as an investment vehicle.

This volatility has made bitcoin virtually useless as a currency. As I have argued, the most effective form of money is that which has no value itself. One dollar is worth one dollar. It may move against another currency or rise or decline in purchasing power, but this is unlikely to mean a radical shift. Speculative booms and falls, as experienced by bitcoin, mean that accepting it in payment is fraught with uncertainty. Its purchasing power may rise or fall dramatically. One bitcoin is not the same as another. Another problem for cryptocurrencies using the block-chain model is that the complexity of the system makes it slow, whereas other payment methods are virtually instantaneous.

The security of cryptocurrencies is also a matter of concern. A weak point lies in the exchanges where they can be bought and sold. The Mt Gox exchange in 2013 saw $350 million worth of bitcoin stolen. Hackers have also discovered ways of finding the codes to individual wallets. At the other end of the spectrum, the anonymity of cryptocurrencies makes them ideal for illegal transactions or avoiding taxation.

One benefit of cryptocurrencies is that they are created and circulated free of debt. Non-miners can obtain the currency by accepting payment in the digital currency or by buying the currency itself. However, it has none of the social and public benefits of public money. While cryptocurrencies, by definition, have a monetary community – people who accept and use them – there is no social identification, as one of the main features is anonymity. Participants hold their currency in computer-based wallets, but there is no way of linking these to individual identities. However, there are groups of people whose common interest is enthusiasm about the potential of cryptocurrency, which does form a social focus.

Cryptocurrencies have the benefit over bank-created money that they are issued free of debt. They can be either earned or bought. However, because they are conceived as a neutral means of exchange they lack a social or public context. Presumably, if they become more prevalent, ways will be found to tax them, but, unlike public currencies, there is no public authority backing the system. As one advertiser acknowledged in the small print, cryptocurrencies rest upon technology and trust. While cryptocurrencies may be lacking social and public elements, there is widespread interest on the part of social and public institutions as to whether the underlying block-chain technology can be applied in other contexts.

While the motivation behind the development of cryptocurrencies was to create an anonymous and autonomous monetary space, free of institutional encumbrance, other approaches to creating money had quite the opposite aim, to build interactive communities.

Communal magic: social money

A very different approach to the creation of non-bank, non-state money is when people create a currency medium for themselves. Major motivations for doing so are a lack of access to the public currency or the desire for some social and/or economic autonomy. What is interesting about such initiatives is that the magic of money can be seen in action. While most forms of social money are small scale, they show the elements of how a money system should or shouldn't work. The simplest form of money system is a babysitting circle (Box 6.1).

Box 6.1: A simple card trick: the babysitting circle

Kate Mc

> A babysitting circle is what the name implies, a group of parents
> who agree to babysit for each other on a reciprocal basis. Babysitting
> circles operate on time-based exchange, usually mediated by tokens.
> The most straightforward way to operate the circle is for someone
> to cut up a sheet of card into small tokens valued at one hour or half
> an hour. These are distributed – for example, ten tokens are given to
> each family.

It would be possible to organise the circle on the basis of simple
reciprocity without the tokens. Each parent would keep track
of what they were 'owed' from the other parents. However,
misunderstandings could easily arise and it would be difficult to
transfer value ('I can't babysit for you tonight but Steve owes me
from last week, so you could try him and say I am transferring
my claim on him to you, but then you will owe me ...').

The use of tokens is much simpler and illustrates the efficacy of
a uniform money. The babysitting circle is a simple social money
system. The tokens are issued free of debt and form the basis for
'trading'. The circle would not work if the tokens were initially
lent to each parent: in the absence of any new tokens coming
into the circle (new members) the tokens would dry up as they
were returned to the 'banker'. It is the debt-free nature of the
original tokens that makes it a sustainable system. What matters
is that there are sufficient tokens to represent the likely level
of activity. In my own experience of babysitting circles, when

families left their tokens were not withdrawn, so the number in circulation gradually expanded as new people came. Nor, as far as I know, did anyone cheat and make their own tokens. What was important was goodwill and access to sufficient babysitters.

The unit of measurement for the babysitting circle is time. Time has long been proposed as the most appropriate basis of a money system. Reformers in the nineteenth century saw time as a fair way of measuring people's work. It was also put forward as a way that workers could organise their own medium of exchange. A founder of the British Co-operative Movement, Robert Owen (1771–1858), proposed a National Equitable Labour Exchange in 1832. A labour currency was printed like a banknote that promised to 'Deliver to the Bearer Exchange Hours to the Value of XX Hours'. Other radicals such as Marx and Proudhon suggested similar ideas.

None of these worked out in practice, but what did work in the nineteenth century was the use by better-paid workers of the money they earned to set up their own economic system of consumer co-operatives. At first they used the money to buy items such as flour in bulk. This was later expanded into the co-operative production of food and other consumer goods, together with a full range of other services, including banking. The Co-operative Movement did not set up its own currency, but funded its expansion through its own bank. Similarly, building societies were set up that could make loans to fund affordable housing, although the amount of new money created through lending was strictly regulated.

The twentieth century saw a resurgence of the time-money idea. In 1992 a book was published by Edgar S. Cahn and Jonathan Rowe whose title is self-explanatory: *Time Dollars: The New Currency That Enables Americans to Turn Their Hidden Resource Time Into Personal Security and Community Renewal.* Unlike the labour currency proposals of the nineteenth century, the Time Dollar movement focused on work outside of the formal economy. It aimed to reach areas of personal and community life that people could control, particularly their own personal time. One of the most successful application of the time-money principle is the Ithaca HOUR, a currency in Ithaca, New York state (Box 6.2).

Box 6.2: Ithaca HOURS

Founded in 1991 by Paul Glover, the project has issued over $100,000 in paper money, creating millions of dollars in trade. The main motivation was to create a currency that would have a positive social and environmental impact. As the Ithaca HOURS website says:

We printed our own money because we watched Federal dollars come to town, shake a few hands, then leave to buy rainforest lumber and fight wars. Ithaca HOURS by contrast, stay in our region to help us hire each other.

The Ithaca HOUR is equated to $10. They are accepted by several hundred businesses, from roofing to restaurants. Ithaca HOURS are put into circulation by an annual payment in HOURS being made to everyone who is listed in the movement's Directory.

Time-based money has also been used extensively in Japan. One of the best-known examples is Fureai Kippu (caring relationship tickets), a wide range of networks set up to provide care for elderly people since 1992. There were approaching four hundred branches in 2012. Care-givers can accumulate healthcare credits for their own use, or they can transfer their credit to others, for example to obtain care for relatives living in another part of the country. While some groups 'pay' exclusively in the form of time credits, some others allow the option of taking a cash payment.

Somewhere between the babysitting circle and the large-scale time-dollar model are LETS (Local Exchange Trading Systems). LETS are membership organisations where people carry out tasks or trade with each other, coordinated by a central record rather than by operating any form of alternative currency. This builds a limiting factor into the structure because, like running a babysitting circle without the tokens, exchange interaction gets quite complex very quickly. A much simpler approach is to create social money.

Alternatives to the official currency have a long, and not always benign, history. 'Scrip' – forms of unofficial money – was abused by employers under the 'truck' system whereby workers were paid in vouchers cashable only in employer-owned shops where prices were high. Loyalty cards and air miles are modern forms of scrip that can be spent only in the sponsoring organisation. A store in my local town, long closed down, created its own coinage tokens that it would give in change. However, most scrip is not created to restrict expenditure but to increase it where there is an insufficient supply of the public currency, which was very much a problem during the Depression (Box 6.3).

Box 6.3: Scrip

Worgl is a small town in Austria that had one third unemployment in 1932. The mayor, Michael Unterguggenberger, created around 10,000 schillings in scrip notes backed by a loan from the local credit union savings bank. Following the principles of Silvio Gesell (1862–1930), the scrip was subject to demurrage – that is, to a decline in value over time. To maintain their original value, the scrip notes had to be stamped for a small fee each month. This was an encouragement to spend the notes quickly, thereby increasing economic activity. The scrip money was a great success. Major public works were carried out and employment increased. The scrip circulated much more quickly than the national currency and unemployment fell by 25%. The money was used to pay the wages of city employees and was in turn accepted in payment of taxes. The scheme was so successful that other towns were planning to follow suit. This alarmed the national government, which closed the project down after a year. Several similar schemes in the US were blocked by the government as it feared that the monetary system was being 'democratised' out of its hands.

Most of the contemporary examples of socially created money are not a response to a collapse of the national currency, but they are often created to energise a flagging local economy. Often referred to as complementary, parallel or local currency, the social money is generally similar in structure and value to the national currency. However, its remit is generally local. Currently one of the most successful alternative currencies operates in a prosperous region of southern Germany.

The chiemgauer social currency is named after a region in Bavaria. Rather unusually, it did not start through the concerns of local citizens about the local economy but as a school project to help students understand how money worked. The project was launched in 2003 and was based on notes valued from one to fifty, with the value pegged to the euro. It started slowly with only 130 people and some local businesses involved, but within a few years had a turnover of over €5 million, with 600 business and 2,500 people regularly using it.

The secret to its success is two-fold. Like the Worgl scrip, the chiemgauer money is time-limited and it has institutional backing. As with most social money, the main aim is to keep trading local. The chiemgauer notes are valid for only three months, encouraging people to use them quickly. They can be renewed up to seven times by buying a stamp worth 2% of the note's value. As a result, the chiemgauer circulates more than twice as quickly as the euro.

The running of the chiemgauer system is paid for by a one-off registration fee of €100 for participating businesses and a monthly charge of €5 to €10, depending on turnover. In return for their payments, businesses are listed in a directory and on the currency's website. Various local agencies and banks also provide interest-free loans to local businesses in chiemgauer. Chiemgauer notes can be changed back into euros, subject to a 5% transaction fee. Sixty per cent of the chiemgauer organisation's income is given to local charities and non-profit organisations. Three per cent of all transactions also goes to charity. Despite its success, the project accounts for only 0.2% of the region's economy.

Like Worgl, institutional support for the chiemgauer came from local credit organisations and the co-operative bank. This enabled the issue of a debit card that could transfer the chiemgauer. Local banks also offered the facility of exchanging euros for chiemgauer. Regional currencies like chiemgauer are also well supported politically in Germany, with more than fifty schemes running or in development. For Worgl, an important aspect of its success was the involvement of local government spending and taxes. In both respects, the UK is not such a supportive environment and it has therefore been less successful in launching local currencies because there is less institutional support.

Money is social and public

The lesson of the three examples of state-free money is that all have their flaws. The euro has found that creating a money system with a solely commercial remit was not feasible. As soon as a crisis came the ECB, after some initial reluctance, had to behave much like a national central bank. It will not be able to return to its original neutral position. The main drawback is that the public currency supply is not safe in the hands of the banking system. The Eurozone will need to face the fact that money requires a political as well as an administrative framework. However, this would require not just administrative rules but a politics of money. How is the ECB to respond to future requests for support? How active is it to be in supporting Eurozone states and economies?

The problems experienced by bitcoin illustrate the limitations of a technical approach to money. It is hard to see how a rudderless, computer-generated system could become a universal currency. The main weakness is its volatility. As I have argued, the most effective form of money is one that does not have its own value, and most certainly not one that changes dramatically. Bitcoin compounds the problem of modern money. It is now well established that public currencies have nothing backing them except the willingness of people to accept them in transfer. Bitcoin adds to this a market value accorded to the bitcoin itself that is backed by nothing but people's willingness to buy and sell it. At least John Law based his paper money on the productivity of France and its colonies (see pages 85–6). Bitcoin as a speculative asset is built on nothing but a computer code.

Social money comes much closer to the idea of money as a social phenomenon. It doesn't pretend to be commercial. Far from being a speculative asset like bitcoin, many forms of social money are structured so as to lose value over time. However, it does not appear that social money initiatives are likely to overtake public currencies in the near future. While in Worgl the local money offered a real challenge to the national currency, this was because it operated very much as a public currency. Council employees were paid in the currency and it could be submitted in taxes. Social currencies that are not linked into the public economy can still have a positive impact. What they can do is encourage more local or more specific economic interaction, such as care provision.

The conclusion from these experiments in building money systems is that money cannot be just administrative and technical, nor can it be just social. Public currencies are just that, public. The way forward is not to abolish the public face of money, nor to deny the sovereign power to create the public currency, but to democratise it. I will make this case in the final chapter.

SEVEN

Breaking the spell: money for the people

I argued at the beginning of this book that there seems to be something magical about money. Like the magician's trick where something seems to be moving independently under a square of cloth, money appears to move around without anyone pulling the strings. However, when the magician shakes the cloth there is nothing there. Similarly, when it is examined more closely, money seems to vanish into thin air. This is particularly true of modern fiat money. It is nothing from nowhere. There are trillions of dollars, pounds, euros and other currencies in bank accounts across the globe that exist only as numbers. There is nothing in the money system 'backing' those numbers. No superior or 'real' form of money. Is this fiat money an illusion, like the magician's sleight of hand?

Is money magic?

The answer must be no. Unless we believe in fairies – or fairy tales. So why does money look and behave like magic? The main reason is its elusive nature. Like a magic trick, it is hard to see how it is done. This is not to imply that there is a magician conjuring the illusion. There is no manipulator behind the curtain – as was the case in *The Wizard of Oz*. If there were, he, she or they would have been discovered (quite literally) by now. Such a magician would have needed to be in place during the emergence of human societies, as all known communities appear to have something that approximates money. All seem to need some tangible or intangible yardstick to act as a comparative measure of value. There is also usually some mechanism to transfer that value around.

I have stressed that the measurement is comparative rather than absolute. Money cannot give *a* value: what is a Yap stone worth, or a Lele cloth? What it can say is that a particular injury or dowry payment is worth this stone rather than that stone, or fifty cloths as against one hundred cloths.

Some of the seeming magic of money is because traditional and historical forms can be enchanting in themselves: gold, silver, stones, shells. Even more magical is money's immateriality in modern economies. Trust in a notional currency (pounds, dollars, euros) represented as paper, base metal or electronic blips enables the provision of goods and services, from personal care to massive infrastructure projects. Money is also imbued with the power of magic: it mesmerises its users so that they accept its organisation and structures without question. There are many phrases that emphasise the power of money. Money talks. The bottom line. Money makes the world go round. It's on the money.

Yet money is not magic. It is a social institution that is ubiquitous in human societies. Using the monetary yardstick – whatever form it takes – value can be determined economically by price on the market, socially by custom or personal choice (how big a gift to give, what injury payment to make) and publicly by political priority and public policy (level of expenditure, fees, fines or tax). People are part of a monetary community if they accept and acknowledge a common yardstick and trust that its representation will be honoured on transfer. What is being trusted is that the shells, coins or bank numbers will be accepted in payment of a debt, be seen as an appropriate gift or spent in a shop.

The power that money has rests in its symbolism. It is not the form that it takes that matters, it is the common acknowledgement that it receives in use. This is illustrated by the very different forms of traditional money, and the way they lost credibility when mass produced, as discussed in Chapter Two. The money object was not honoured in itself as a type of stone or shell, but as local communities' *version* of those things. It was the history and symbolism of the object that mattered. This could not be reproduced just by creating seemingly identical stones or shells. Similarly, coins were not just lumps of metal, they were stamped with the symbolism of the ruling power. As money became made of more mundane materials they often carried a physical representation of traditional forms of money. For example, the early Chinese paper money made from mulberry bark had at its centre images of strings of cash metal discs.

Modern fiat money is no less symbolic. The euro banknote is as simple as money can be. It is a piece of paper with a number on it. It makes no promises, and states no conditions for its use. Yet it is not just any piece of paper. It is recognised and used by millions of people. It is the medium with which people establish their entitlements and obligations: how much is my labour worth, what taxes do I owe, how much is that hat? However, money is not a passive medium. Nor does money flow around under its own logic. Money is created, circulated and allocated by human agency. It is not nothing from nowhere. It is something from somewhere. Decisions are made as to what is valued in money terms: elite football is well rewarded, particularly in the UK; care work is largely unpaid or low paid.

The critical area I have addressed in this book is how fiat money is created. It comes from nowhere in the sense that there are no money mines or money trees; but new banknotes and new numbers in bank accounts have an origin. I have identified these as bank lending and state spending. Both have a critical impact on the way we live our lives. To be able to bring these questions into critical debate I first had to break the spell of fairy-tale thinking.

Myths and tales

A central aim of this book has been to explode the myths about money that stem from a conventional market perspective. Chapter One set out the key ideas of this approach to money in the form of a fairy tale. While some of the tale was true, there were two total myths that have had a major impact on mainstream theories and policies around money. These myths are the idea that money emerged from a previous market economy based on barter and that this original form of money was precious-metal coinage. Both ideas are false because there is no evidence of widespread barter before markets based on money developed, and precious-metal coinage emerged long before market economies. There are also many forms of money other than precious-metal coins.

Seeing money as a by-product of the market system limits its main function to enabling efficient exchange. Money is perceived as a purely technical instrument that reflects the underlying economy. The ideal money is one that mirrors exactly the value of the goods and services exchanged, either by being made of something valuable in itself like gold or silver, or by being limited in total volume to the minimum necessary to secure market activity. The idea that money originated in precious metal led to the assumption that money is something that should be treated as rare and valuable. Despite the fact that modern money is neither, it is still held to be in short supply. Firms are seen as competing for funds. State spending is decried as reducing the amount of money available for market investment. Money is assumed to be zero sum. Your welfare payment is my taxes. As I argued earlier, this builds social conflict into the heart of the modern money supply.

The idea that money originated in the market-place also led to the assumption that the only source of monetary wealth was the market. This completely ignores the long history of rulers and elites in the history of money. As we saw in Chapter Three, the early precious-metal coinage was monopolised by rulers and mainly used in a military or diplomatic context. The weakness for the ruler in adopting precious-metal money was the need to maintain constant supplies of the metal. For this reason, rulers also used other forms of money such as paper, base metal or tally sticks.

The variety of money forms developed by early states gives a completely different history to money from the precious metal story. As discussed in Chapter Three, the state theory of money focused not on the market but the role of state authority in the circulation of money, particularly the power to tax. Whatever form of money states adopted to fund their expenditure, people had to have access to that money in order to pay their taxes. This could be achieved by providing labour or goods to the state, or to someone else who could pay in the relevant currency. In Chapter Two it was noted how colonial powers harnessed the labour of the colonised by demanding tax payments in the colonial currency.

The most important aspect of precious-metal money was that it did not transfer a symbol or representation of value. It transferred a value in its own right through its value as a commodity. I have argued that this makes it less useful as a money. There is less incentive to transfer it and it is necessary to have another yardstick against which to establish the value of the metal. As we saw with the gold standard, the value of paper money in terms of gold was fixed by agents of the state, not by the market.

The myths also ignored the social history of money in non-market, non-state societies. Far from originating in market exchange, money took very different forms and was used for a range of purposes. It cemented social relationships through gifts and tribute. It marked life stages: birth, puberty, marriage, death. It enabled access to cultural groupings such as membership of secret societies. It maintained social cohesion through injury payments, and as peace offerings it avoided inter-group conflict.

From this wider perspective on money it cannot be seen as a passive technical instrument of the market. It is an active institution in human societies that is socially and historically constructed. Far from being limited to a market function, money establishes comparative values in a range of circumstances – social, political and economic.

Peeling back the curtain

The basic definition of money in this book is that it is a comparative measure of value that enables the representative transfer of that value. I have argued that money is most effective in carrying out those roles if it has no value in itself, if it is merely a numerical scale (five, ten, twenty pounds, dollars, euros). This is the case for modern fiat money, which does not have any intrinsic value. There is nothing backing it other than the willingness of people to acknowledge the relative value it represents.

Money is therefore social to its core. It also rests on public authority. In the example of the collapse of the Northern Rock bank in Chapter Five, neither the head of the bank nor the governor of the Bank of England could halt the run. Only when the government treasurer, the Chancellor of the Exchequer, put the government's promise behind the bank, did the people disperse.

Money is therefore also political to the core. Both the social and the political promise of money come before its economic role. This was shown to be the case for both the euro and cryptocurrencies in the previous chapter. The ECB could not avoid working directly with states to stabilise the banking system, and where cryptocurrencies have become speculative commodities this has rendered them virtually useless as money.

In recognising and honouring a particular notional money, users form a monetary community. This may or may not overlap with other social groupings. A token-using babysitting circle is a tightly knit monetary community. Similarly, most nation-states have their own distinct currency. The Eurozone has a geographic identity. Looser networks do not have an identity other than to honour a particular currency, such as those who trade globally in dollars. However, they all have the same institutional structure: they recognise a comparative notional measure of value, together with an acknowledged and authorised means of transferring that value.

Are there no magic money trees?

I have described modern fiat money as nothing from nowhere. Yet it has a structure as a social institution. Somehow nothing from nowhere becomes something from somewhere. That looks like magic. Who or what has the power to make nothing into something? Certainly you or I don't. If people like you and me produced notes or coins or set up a bank in our back yard we would quickly be arrested and charged with counterfeiting and fraud. Money is not only a social institution, it is a public institution. As I have stressed many times, it is not the form of the money that matters, it is the symbolism it represents.

For most people there will be only one form of money – the public currency. When the British prime minister said there were no magic money trees, she meant there was no source of new publicly available money. She was wrong. There are (at least) two: banks and states.

Banks create money when they lend

Fairy tales take a long time to evaporate. The myth that banks act only as a link between savers and borrowers was not finally refuted until the second decade of the twenty-first century, when leading monetary institutions such as the US Federal Reserve, the Bank of England and the International Monetary Fund acknowledged that banks were creating new public currency when they made loans. The policy implications of the public currency being created out of nowhere and lent to borrowers on a purely commercial basis have still not been taken on board.

We have already seen in Chapter Four how banks create new public currency. They do not mint coins or print public currency banknotes (except under licence from the central bank). What they can do is make loans in the public currency by setting up new bank numbers in bank accounts. As has already been pointed out, no other depositors lose numbers from their bank accounts in the process. Banks are therefore creating money out of thin air when they make loans. But they are not making just any money: when banks make loans they are putting new public currency money into circulation. Conventional banking theory tried hard to say that this was not really the public currency, it was only 'credit' money. This illusion was shattered by the 2007–08 crisis when some governments had to guarantee all bank accounts. With transactions increasingly becoming cashless, bank and other forms of transfer are clearly as real as any other form of money. A bank account transfer is seen as being no different to a cash payment.

As discussed in Chapter Four, bank lending has effectively privatised the creation of the public currency supply. Every time a new loan is taken out, new public currency is created. The public currency is a network of promises that we will all acknowledge each other's transfer of those promises when they are presented. Nothing holds those promises together, except that acknowledgment.

What is distinctive about bank-created money is that it is issued and circulated through debt. As the illustration shows, bank-created money flows in a circuit.

Figure 7.1: Bank money circuit

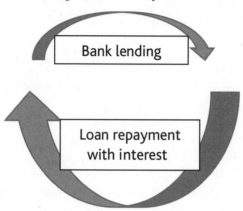

Money is lent by the bank and returned by the borrower with interest. Loans put new money into the economy. Loan repayments remove money from circulation. You will notice that the bottom arrow is larger than the top arrow. Banks are potentially removing more money from the economy than they lend. This is because the loans are repaid with interest. As long as the circuit is flowing well, and preferably expanding with increased lending, there will be no problem in repaying loans with interest. However, if loans remain steady and there is no independent source of money, there is a problem of where the money to pay the interest will come from. More importantly, if there are no new borrowers the money supply will quickly contract as old loans are repaid. Debt is therefore not a good basis for the supply of money. As the crisis showed, when loans dry up, so does the supply of public currency.

Economically, basing a money supply on borrowing is always threatened by crisis if governments, businesses and citizens can take no more debt. As discussed in Chapter Four, a money supply based on debt is also socially problematic because it will favour the wealthy rather than the poor. The main criterion for a loan is that the proposed expenditure is viable and the borrower is credit-worthy. The poor are unlikely to score on either count. Money must therefore gravitate towards the better-off. Creating money through debt may also drive unsustainable growth, whether economically or ecologically.

The democratic challenge must be: by what right are the banks creating the public currency as debt? To whom are the banks accountable for being able to create currency out of nothing? Who are the beneficiaries of this largesse? Should bank lending continue to be seen as a private matter? As they are exercising the sovereign power to create money, should banks be seen as an arm of the state and be made democratically answerable? Should all banks be nationalised or socialised? Should their power to create money through debt be removed? Should they continue to be bailed out by the state if they end up in a crisis?

All these questions, and many more, become relevant if the role of banks in creating the public money supply is recognised. What has become fused is the centrality of credit to capitalism (where bank lending plays a key role) and the control of the public money supply. As we saw in Chapter Five, bank loans as 'leverage' fuel the financial markets. Borrowing from the banks funds speculative gambles, buyouts and takeovers, the latter often leaving the targeted companies burdened with debt. Borrowing has become a way of life in modern economies, from mortgages to student and consumer loans. Bank loans are involved in most commercial transactions. No one orchestrated the slipping of the money supply into speculative debt, but the consequences are deeply troubling. Modern economies are mired in debt, but under the spell of neoliberal handbag economics they ignore, even deride, the one source of debt-free money – the state.

States create money when they spend

In most economies it is exclusively the state that has the formal power to create and circulate money. Yet, according to the fairy tale in Box 1.1, money is created by the market and the role of the state in the creation of money is largely ignored. As noted earlier, according to neoliberal ideology, states should be prevented from creating money because this is deemed to be detrimental to the market, most notably by leading to inflation.

Seeing the origin of money in the market leads to the claim that the state is continually raiding the pockets of the 'wealth creators', stealing the 'tax-payers' money' instead of leaving it in (their) pockets. Every penny that the state spends is seen as a burden on the market. Despite the claims and strictures of neoliberal ideology, states do 'print money' in two ways. First, it is produced out of thin air by the central bank to provide cash and support for the money-creating activities of the banking sector, as was made explicit in the process of quantitative easing.

Second, money is created and circulated as the government spends, in the same way as banks create money as they lend. When banks lend money they add to the overall money supply; when that money is repaid, the debt is cancelled and the money supply is reduced. States spend money and then offset it against tax and other income received. As with bank lending, the state drawing up and allocating a budget is an act of money creation. Public spending adds to the money supply, while taxation removes money from circulation. Like bank lending and repayment, public spending and tax-raising are in a continuous circuit.

Figure 7.2: Public money circuit

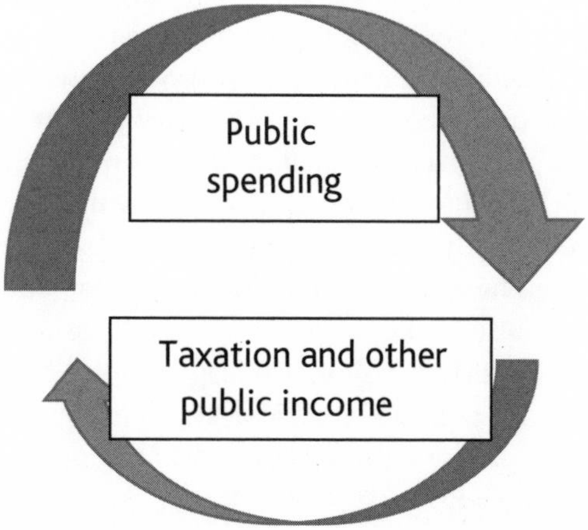

How the circuit operates and what is seen as the driving element depends on how the public-spending circuit is perceived. Money is flowing in and out. If the driving force is seen as the raising of taxes it will be assumed that public spending is dependent upon the tax take. If public spending is seen as the driving force, the ability to pay taxes will depend on access to public money in the first place.

Several factors indicate that state spending comes before taxation. First is the existence of deficit. This could not occur if expenditure waited upon tax receipts and only spent what was in the 'pot'. Also a substantial portion of the tax take comes from people and organisations in the public sector, directly or indirectly. They could not pay their taxes unless they had first been paid from the public budget. Nor could all the money to fund the public sector come from the private sector. Public economies are too big to be funded entirely by the 'wealth-creating' sector as the neoliberals claim. In 1995 Germany's public expenditure was nearly 60% of GDP, and in Britain during the two world wars expenditure went up to over 70%. Even the low public expenditure of the US reached 45% following the 2007–08 crisis.

States do not check their tax accounts *before* they spend. The balance between public expenditure and public income becomes clear only *after* the expenditure has taken place. The political choice is then what is to be done with any 'deficit' – that is, surplus expenditure over income, represented by the larger arrow in Figure 7.2. The extra money could be left to flow around the economy (if there were no inflationary pressures). It could be seen as a perennial 'overdraft' at the national bank. Or the money to bridge the deficit could be met by increased taxes or be borrowed from the financial sector, thereby increasing the national debt. The way the deficit is addressed is a political choice reflecting the way money is perceived. If all money is seen as coming from the private sector, handbag economics would argue that the state has exceeded its house-keeping allowance, which must be repaid. If the state is seen as an independent monetary actor there is no automatic debt to the market.

What is important is that states have the sovereign power to create money free of debt. As with bank lending, this power can always be abused, but that is no reason to deny that it exists. If the money which the banks lend and the money which the states spend comes from nowhere, if it is just new numbers, the fundamental question must be: who determines how that power to create money is allocated and used? In this final chapter I want to look at two proposals that seek to democratise money. One is to make money widely available as a social resource. The other is to make money subject to democratic control. Both are ways of putting money into people's hands. The aim must be to restore the sovereign power over money not to rulers, but to the democratic sovereign, the people.

Giving money to the people

Access to money is essential in modern economies where nearly all aspects of sustenance need to be bought. The main means of access to money for most people are earnings or welfare payments of some sort. Borrowing can increase the current availability of money, but it needs future income to pay it back. The disadvantage of relying on earnings for money is that the type of work may be exploitative, dangerous, uncertain, unpleasant, unnecessary or unfulfilling. Those relying on welfare payments are often stigmatised as lazy scroungers. A basic income is seen as a solution to both problems. It could free people from the need to work and, since it is provided for everyone, there is no stigma attached to it. However, the case for a basic income is more fundamental than avoiding unpleasant and unnecessary work or social stigma. It is about a human right to livelihood.

A basic income represents the unconditional right of all members of a community to share in the benefits of the society. The idea goes back a long way. The Romans had a 'dole' which was a distribution of bread to the citizens. Thomas More (1478–1535) in his book *Utopia* promotes a minimum income as a solution to the prevalence of theft and the severe punishment of thieves, including by death. If people were stealing only because they had no other access to food, it made more sense to feed them than to hang them.

The moral and political case for a universal payment was made by Thomas Paine (1737–1809), who argued that the earth was a common heritage for everyone and that each should have their share. Paine's argument was that private ownership of land meant that the people as a whole lost access to their share of the earth. Private owners should therefore pay a ground-rent to the rest of the populace to compensate for this loss. This money would be put into a fund that would pay everyone at the age of twenty-one a one-off endowment, which at the time, 1796, he suggested would be £15. He also put forward the idea of a basic income whereby people aged over fifty would be paid £10 per year.

Over the next two hundred years such proposals resurfaced many times, making the case that all citizens should share in the productivity of both land and people. Concepts such as social dividend, national dividend, social credit, captured the idea of land and resources being held in common. However, such universal ideas did not make much headway, unlike the more conditional payments associated with the growth of welfare states. National insurance systems based on prior contributory payments and welfare payments based on need also undermined the idea of universality. One example of the issue of a citizen dividend along the lines of Paine's idea of a common heritage comes from Alaska. In 1976 a Permanent Fund was set up from income generated by the sale of Alaska's natural resources, mainly petroleum. The fund pays an annual dividend to eligible residents. The highest amount paid was over $2,000 in 2008.

A completely different argument for a universal payment came not from the radical thinking of writers such as Paine, but from neoclassical economics and the logic of the market. As we have seen, the problem of debt-based money is that the money supply increases rapidly when borrowers and investors are optimistic, but can go into sharp decline if confidence starts to ebb. What happens then is that public money comes to the fore. This creates a double problem for free-market economists.

The first problem is that because free marketeers see all money as coming from the market, any increase in state spending must mean a growth in state debt which will eventually have to be repaid through taxation. Second, the state will have to make a decision about how to spend or allocate that money. This interferes with the 'free' operation of the market. The solution to this dilemma, put forward by the right-wing economist Milton Friedman, was to deliver the money to the market on a universal basis as 'helicopter money'. Examples of universal payments to counter the effects of the 2007–08 crisis were in Hong Kong, which made a one-off payment of HK$6,000 to all adult residents in 2012, and in Australia, which made a range of one-off allowances and payments, including AU$900 to single-income families, in 2009. The Bush administration in the US responded to the crisis through a one-off tax refund.

An extreme example of issuing helicopter money was the approach of the US victors in the Iraq war. The US administrators were reported as turning all existing assets of the previous regime into US dollar bills – $12 billion worth. These were then distributed into the economy in such an uncontrolled manner that it all disappeared within twelve months without any clear indication of what happened to it.

A citizen income can be seen as the most direct form of economic democracy, which puts financial decisions into people's hands. This does not necessarily mean that people will adopt less consumer-based and income-seeking lifestyles, as some reformers hope. Perhaps like the Iraqi $12 billion, the money will just trickle away. It is also unclear how public services and infrastructure would be organised. Other limitations are that the amount paid might not be sufficient to make a material difference to people's lives or to address inequality. From a handbag economics perspective, a basic income must come from a limited public expenditure pot. This means that, rather than being based on the creation of new public money, existing benefits would need to be 'rolled up' into the universal payment. This would very likely mean that those with the most needs might end up receiving a reduced income. A further problem is eligibility: who counts as a citizen?

A more targeted distribution of money has recently been adopted as a solution to poverty and to aid community development. For more than twenty years from the mid-1970s, poverty was addressed by seeking to integrate poor communities into the market through local enterprise development. In line with market thinking, money was issued as debt disbursed through micro-credit finance. This was based on the encouraging experience of Mohammad Yunus in Bangladesh when, in 1976, he lent a small amount to some women. It appeared that entrepreneurial magic was beginning to work: there were very few defaults and the borrowers prospered. As with all debt-led booms, the first borrowers did well, but over time communities became too heavily indebted. Interest rates were often high, as they included administration and training costs.

By the early 2000s states such as Brazil, Mexico, Indonesia and South Africa were providing poor communities with direct money payments. Evidence began to build that dispensing money free of debt was more successful than micro-credit in eliminating poverty. However, to be effective the distribution of the money needed to be seen as fair in allocation, to be regular and assured, to be substantial enough to make a difference and to be well administered. As Hanlon et al conclude, 'to reduce poverty and promote development, just give money to the poor'.[1]

At the time of writing, experiments with basic income payments are ongoing in Finland, Spain and Canada. The Finnish experiment was launched in January 2017. Over two years, it provided two thousand unemployed people between the ages of twenty-five and fifty-eight with a monthly income of €560 (£475), to be paid even if they found work. It was intended, if successful, to extend the experiment to those in work. However, the project will no longer be funded after the two years are up and the government has instead legislated to make the unemployed take some work or training.

The major problem with basic income proposals is that they may empower individuals but they don't address the wider politics of money. This would require a direct democratic input.

Democratising money

The 2007–08 crisis clearly showed that maintaining the public currency is a public responsibility. If it is a public responsibility, public money should be seen as a public resource. I have identified two sources of new public currency: bank lending and state spending. Both need to be the subject of democratic debate.

If money can be easily created out of nothing, why are governments and the people shackled in debt? Why can't the people create money for themselves free of debt? Why can't money be circulated in a not-for-profit social or public sector?

Why base economic analysis on the butcher, the baker and the candlestick-maker and the hidden hand of the market and not the doctor, the teacher, the care-worker, the artist and the hidden hand of the solidarity economy?

One of the main benefits of the present system, claimed by neoliberalism, is that a market-based system is free of state intervention. Proponents of social and local economies also tend to have a suspicion of the state. For this reason, a bank-led system, despite all the problems of debt-based money, is better than a system depending on a corrupt and authoritarian state. It is true that many states have proved to be inefficient, corrupt and autocratic. Proposals to return the money supply to the state would not be acceptable unless it was fundamentally democratic. It cannot be assumed that public authorities would necessarily use money wisely, unless they were subject to democratically based mandates and effective public scrutiny. Exclusive control of the money supply must not simply be left in the hands of the government in power, or the state apparatus. The public creation and circulation of money must be transparent and accountable.

However, the bank-led money supply is equally problematic. Apart from being debt based it is fundamentally undemocratic and crisis ridden. Also, the case I am making is not that the state *should* create money through public spending; it is that the state *does* create money through public expenditure. What is missing is any democratic debate about the power of banks to privatise the public money supply and the need for states to recognise their monetary autonomy. I would go so far as to say that states are not dependent upon the market for money; it is the market that is dependent upon state money. With the state's reclaiming of the public right to create its own money in its own name for public purposes, the power of banks to create new money could be removed or refocused.

The democratisation of the public money supply could enable new priorities to be set. For example, women's unpaid domestic labour could be recognised; care provision could be seen as a major source of employment. Environmental strategies could be funded, such as providing an 'income' for nature to support its sustainability. How could the supply and use of money be opened to public debate?

Opening the debate

It needs to be recognised that we start from a very low base in our understanding of money. The first stage must be awareness of the role of the state and the banks in the creation and circulation of money. Money can no longer be seen as a private matter between banks and their clients. The security of the public currency is a public responsibility, as shown by the post-crisis bailouts.

The public currency should be seen as a public resource and therefore made subject to decisions about who controls it and how. The market could not exist without bank lending, but it needs to be acknowledged that this creates new money. The state's ability to create money also needs to be acknowledged, as well as the pretence that it is reliant on 'borrowing' or 'taxing'. Both borrowing and taxing are ways of retrieving money from the economy. State borrowing is often described euphemistically as 'sterilising' public spending – that is, taking out of the economy through state debt money equivalent to state expenditure. The question then is: should the wealthy return more money to the state through taxes, rather than gaining an investment by buying state debt?

Political parties would need to put forward their proposals for how they saw the balance between state creation of the money supply and bank creation. Banks would need to be publicly accountable for any currency-creating powers they were given. There would also need to be a debate about ownership of the banks and whether they should be seen as public utilities.

A people's budget

I have argued that a public budget is an act of money creation. There is no 'natural' monetary limit on public expenditure. The question 'where is the money to come from?' is irrelevant. The money comes from nowhere. This is not to say that there are no limits to public capacity, but they are not monetary. Lack of available labour and resources would be obvious examples.

In most societies there will be untapped social and public needs. These could be articulated by citizen and user-producer forums. There will also be areas in which people will want less expenditure. These inputs would need to be amalgamated into local, regional and national budgets. As this would be a complex process, the money allocation and budgets should be for at least a five-year period, with a small margin for interim adjustments. The immediate result of such a system would undoubtedly be a massive jump in public expenditure requests. As this would be a transitioning process, the increase would need to be phased in over a number of years, subject to resource and labour capacity.

A participatory and transparent approach to budgetary decision-making would safeguard against domination by any particular group or body. Setting long-term budgets would mean that governments could not substantially amend proposed levels of money creation during the run-up to elections.

While there is no natural shortage of money for public spending, there is the problem of issuing too much money. A high level of public expenditure could cause inflation by creating a money flow that overwhelmed finite real capacity, particularly in the market sector. I have already argued that taxation and other state income does not *raise* the money to spend, it *retrieves* the money already spent. The role of taxation is to remove excess money. Higher spending need not necessarily mean high taxes if there is slack in the market sector. However, if the market sector is overheating with inflationary pressures there may be a case for extracting more tax than is spent.

However, it is important to recognise that inflationary pressures do not affect only the price of bread. Inflation applies just as much to the stratospheric level of executive pay, stock market hikes and the overheating of financial markets looking for speculative deals. The huge size of global derivative trading – effectively gambling – is several times larger than the production of goods and services. Much of the money generated by bank lending and state spending in recent years has gravitated to the financial sector and hi-tech companies. This makes retrieval of that money much more difficult. The danger is that taxation pressures will fall on more captive groups such as public and private sector employees. Rather than being seen as major contributors to the economy, large tax-avoiding and speculative companies should be seen as a drain on the public resource of money.

The calculation of the likely impact of public expenditure on the overall money supply (in all sectors) would require technical expertise. This is no different from the current situation, where monetary-policy experts aim to avoid inflation and other pressures. A monetary assessment would need to be made to indicate the level of monetary retrieval needed for a particular level of public expenditure, to be raised through taxation and other government charges. The monetary assessors would have no role in determining how much public expenditure there would be or how the taxes would be applied. This is a very different view of the balance between state expenditure and taxes from that of handbag economics. Neoliberals seek to reduce public expenditure to 'balance' tax income. The balance I am talking about here is between public expenditure and economic capacity. Taxation is an instrument of that balance.

The final focus of democratic participation would be the efficiency and efficacy of public spending. Citizens and worker and user groups would monitor public spending on a regular basis. All public and private organisations that received a direct or indirect allocation of public money would need to have clear mechanisms for democratic accountability and transparency in place. Democratising money as proposed here sees the sovereign people making payments to themselves for services to themselves through a vibrant public economy and returning that money to themselves through taxation.

Evidence that participatory budgeting is feasible was demonstrated by the experience of Porto Alegre in Brazil. An initiative of the Brazilian Workers' Party, the system of participatory budgeting was launched in 1989, whereby grassroots assemblies of citizens determined public spending priorities. The assemblies then elected budget delegates to put these proposals forward to higher levels of decision-making. Since that time, more than two thousand examples of participatory budgeting have been explored or established in all parts of the globe.

Money: an alternative story

The story of money in this book starts in the mists of time. We do not know when human communities started comparing value and using objects or ideas symbolically to represent those values and enable comparisons. What has been learned from those who have studied the anthropological evidence is that such symbolic structures exist very widely. As these societies have no state and no market their symbolic means of measuring and transferring value are not set by rulers or used widely in market-like activities. Both the form of the money symbol and its usage are based on custom. This does not mean that there is no change over time, but there is no guiding hand. Money symbolism is a social structure that evolves as a social process.

The ubiquity and antiquity of money reveal it to be one of the most important social institutions. Like culture and religion, it appears to meet some need in human beings or human society. In the case of money, this does not imply some primary economic drive. My reading of the anthropological literature presented in Chapter Two indicates that traditional forms of money were rarely used in anything that approximated to market exchange. Money symbols seem to be used mainly to smooth social relationships and avoid conflict.

Active involvement in the creation and circulation of money symbols emerges with the development of states. Some early states quite literally used a symbol to indicate value: the image of crops or animals or a hieroglyphic representation. They also began the process of trying to tie the money form to a specific product, such as a measure of barley. In the long history of the development of states and markets, money appears in many different forms, from shells to sticks. A major development for Europe was the invention of precious-metal coinage.

Precious-metal coinage appeared to resolve the problem of the symbolism of money. It not only allowed a numerical means of comparison – so many coins of a specified value – it also embodied that value. However, establishing and maintaining the specific value of the coins proved problematic. Also, like in the ancient societies, money, whatever form it took, was not predominantly directed towards market activities. This was the age of the ruler, landed elites and the warlord. Vast amounts of money were used in warfare, building defensive structures and diplomacy. Trade often required obtaining permission from local rulers.

The world of the fairy story in Chapter One emerged only in very recent times – the butcher, the baker, the candlestick-maker trading freely using coins. These certainly would not be made of precious metal, which was too valuable to be useful in daily trading. Local markets used base-metal coin, tally sticks or, more likely, 'tabs' – running accounts that were settled when conditions allowed. As market exchange slowly shifted the structure of the economy away from the dominance of rulers and feudal patterns of production, new means of accounting and transfer saw the development of structures of commercial finance and modern banking based on the activities of traders as described in Chapter Four.

The high point of the world of the fairy story is neoliberalism. The market reigns supreme as the source of all economic value and the means of measuring that value – money. However, as we saw in Chapter Five, money ceased to be the measure of value and became, once more, valued in itself. The aim was not to provide goods and services for the people, but to accumulate money. From the perspective of neoliberalism this was the same thing. Accumulating money is taken to mean that useful economic value had been created.

It may have occurred to the perceptive reader that this story of money looks very like the history of the economy as set out by Karl Marx: customary money in ancient societies (primitive communism), ruler-dominated money (feudalism), market-dominated money (capitalism). This was not my intention. I did not start my twenty-year study of money with that model in mind. I just wanted to know the answer to the question 'Where's the money to come from?' that is used as a way of rejecting progressive ideas. This led to the question 'What is money anyway?'. Like all radical critiques, there followed a process of questioning existing ideas about money and exploring them in the light of available evidence.

What emerged was a three-fold history of money that challenged the ideology of handbag economics and its market fundamentalism. Unlike Marx's three stages, I don't see them as transcending each other. They are all still with us. Money is still used in a non-market context as gifts, charity, membership, compensation, funding. The sovereign power to create money is also still with us. I have made the case that the state continually creates money when it spends, which it retrieves when it taxes. Similarly, banks create money when they lend.

What I want to do is take the magic out of money – to break the spell. The fact that money is essentially nothing from nowhere is not a magician's trick, it is a point of freedom. How can we be constrained by nothing from nowhere? When the question is put 'Where is the money to come from?', we can say it doesn't need to come from anywhere. Money is a vital social institution that is not magic, it is a real social agent that is driven by human actions. It can be willed into existence. That is what banks and states do all the time. They are exercising the sovereign power to create money. In modern democracies the sovereign is the people. Money is not a thing; it is a network of promises and obligations, the minimum of which is that those promises and obligations are honoured. Who is making those promises and obligations in whose name is the fundamental question. The sovereign power of money creation needs to rest with the people so that they can provide the answer.

Notes

Introduction
[1] Quiggin (1949, p 1)

Chapter One
[1] Mankiw and Taylor (2017, p 553)
[2] Menger (1892)

Chapter Two
[1] Quiggin (1949, p 5)
[2] Quiggin (1949, p 322)
[3] Quiggin (1949, p 2)

Chapter Three
[1] Goetzman (2016, p 157)
[2] Desan (2014)
[3] Luke 20: 20–26; Matthew 22: 21.
[4] Knapp (1924, p 1)
[5] Knapp (1924, p 56)

Chapter Five
[1] Greenspan (2008, pp 193–5)
[2] Zuckerman and Strasburg (2010)
[3] Reinhart and Rogoff (2010)
[4] Herndon, Ash and Pollin (2014)

Chapter Seven
[1] Hanlon et al (2010, pp 178–9)

References

Desan, Christine (2014) *Making Money: Coin, Currency and the Coming of Capitalism*, Oxford University Press, Oxford.

Goetzmann, William N. (2016) *Money Changes Everything*, Princeton University Press, Princeton NJ.

Greenspan, Alan (2008) *The Age of Turbulence*, Penguin, London.

Hanlon, Joseph, Armando Barrientos and David Hulme (2010) *Just Give Money to the Poor: The Development Revolution from the Global South*, Kumerian Press, Sterling VA.

Herndon, Thomas, Michael Ash and Robert Pollin (2014) 'Does High Public Debt Consistently Stifle Economic Growth? A Critique of Reinhart and Rogoff', *Cambridge Journal of Economics* 38 (2), pp 257–279.

Knapp, G.F. (1924) *The State Theory of Money*, Macmillan, London.

Mankiw, N. Gregory and Mark P. Taylor (2017) *Economics*, Cengage Learning EMEA, Andover, UK.

Menger, C. (1892) 'On the Origin of Money', *Economic Journal* 2, pp 238–255.

Quiggin, Alison Hingston (1949) *A Survey of Primitive Money*, Methuen and Co. Ltd, London, https://archive.org/stream/surveyofprimitiv033390mbp/surveyofprimitiv033390mbp_djvu.txt (accessed 27 March 2018).

Reinhart, Carmen and Kenneth Rogoff (2010) 'Growth in Time of Debt', NBER Working Paper 15639, January 2010, http://www.nber.org/papers/w15639.

Zuckerman, Gregory and Jenny Strasburg (2010) 'Banks' Loans to Funds are Back at Levels Before Crisis', *Wall Street Journal*, 9 January, https://www.wsj.com/articles/SB10001424052748703535104574646710848896566 (accessed 14 February 2018).

Annotated bibliography

Dodd, Nigel (1994) *The Sociology of Money*, **Polity, Cambridge.**
Nigel Dodd's book stands out as an early sociological work addressing money as a social phenomenon in the modern era. This is a largely theoretical text drawing on the work of major social theorists including Marx, Simmel, Parsons and Habermas, as well as more recent currents of thought such as poststructuralism. Dodd follows Knapp in seeing the state as playing a major – though not always successful – role in maintaining the money system. His conclusion is that money is a slippery concept whose essential nature is 'indeterminacy' and, as such, its functioning rests on trust. His book is ground breaking in showing how important the study of money is for social theory and how important sociological analysis is for the study of money.

Davies, Glynn (2002) *A History of Money* **(3rd edition), University of Wales Press, Cardiff.**
A must-read book for anyone interested in the history of money. Davies has meticulously presented the history of money from ancient states to the introduction of the euro. While the British experience is central, a wide range of other monetary histories are presented.

Graeber, David (2011) *Debt: The First 5,000 Years*, **Melville House Publishing, New York.**
Although this book is titled 'Debt' it also develops a view of money much in line with the other radical critiques presented here. As Graeber is an anthropologist he is very informative on non-market, non-state economies and the role of traditional money, including a detailed analysis of Mary Douglas's study

of Lele cloth money as discussed in Chapter Two of this book. Graeber is very helpful in providing an extensive discussion of the social uses of traditional money, including wergild (blood money). However, as well as his detailed exploration of the anthropological literature, Graeber also presents a history of money that sees it alternating between eras when the desire to have money with intrinsic value is prevalent and periods where money is a more socially grounded token.

Ingham, Geoffrey (2004) *The Nature of Money*, **Polity, Cambridge.**

This is a key text in the sociological exploration of money. The first part covers similar ground to this book in subjecting orthodox conventional thinking on money to radical critiques. Ingham explores the work of major classical social theorists such as Marx, Weber and Simmel, as well as more contemporary theories of money. The second half of the book covers similar ground to the history of money in this book, focusing mainly on the emergence of what Ingham calls capitalist credit-money. Like this book, he looks at developments current at the time of writing, including new technologies of money, social money and the euro. In concluding that money is a social construction he leaves open the political implications.

Jackson, Andrew and Ben Dyson (2012) *Modernising Money*, **Positive Money, London.**

This is a policy-oriented book that makes the case for monetary reform. The argument made here is supported by a widespread social movement known in Britain as Positive Money. The aim of the movement, and the book, is to inform legislators and the public about the nature of money through an analysis and critique of the bank-led creation of money. The book opens with a short critique of the conventional view of money originating in barter, before presenting a critical analysis of the present money and banking system. Jackson and Dyson then go on to recount the economic, social and environmental consequences of the current debt-based money system. The final section proposes reforming the money supply through removing the ability of the banks to create money. The role of the banks would be replaced by an independent Monetary Creation Committee that would respond to market conditions. This differs from my proposal, discussed in Chapter Seven of this book, which aims to democratise the creation of money.

Martin, Felix (2014) *Money: The Unauthorised Biography*, Vintage, London.

Although Martin's background is in economics and banking, including a stint at the World Bank and work in the financial sector, this book is probably the nearest in structure and content to this book. It is very readable and accessible. In addressing the nature of money and the history of money, Martin expands the analysis made in this book quite substantially, drawing on an extensive and wide-ranging literature. He is particularly good on the transition from sovereign money to bank-led money as discussed here in Chapters Three and Four. Other substantial sections in Martin's book relevant to these two chapters are the debate about the gold standard and the John Law experiment in France. He comes to similar radical conclusions that the current money system cannot be defended.

Mellor, Mary (2010) *The Future of Money: From Financial Crisis to Public Resource*, Pluto, London.

This is the first book in which I made the case for seeing money as a public resource. It addresses the theory of money and the emergence of a debt-based, bank-led economy. The book explores the link between credit and capitalism, the financialisation and globalisation of the economy, the prevalence of debt and the privatisation of the money supply. The 2007–08 financial crisis and its aftermath are discussed in detail and the case for taking public control of the money system is made.

Mellor, Mary (2015) *Debt or Democracy: Public Money for Sustainability and Social Justice*, Pluto, London.

The focus of this book is public money and the case for recognising a public economy monetarily independent of the market. It introduces my critique of neoliberal handbag economics and makes the case for democratising the money supply as discussed here in Chapter Seven. The ongoing consequences of the financial crisis are picked up from where *The Future of Money* left off, including austerity and bank rescue. In particular, the role of the myths of conventional economics in driving policy options is critiqued. Proposals for democratising money are set in the context of rethinking economic concepts. In place of production, market and profit, *Debt or Democracy* proposes principles of sustainability, provisioning and social justice.

Pettifor, Ann (2017) *The Production of Money: How to Break the Power of the Bankers*, Verso, London.

Like Jackson and Dyson, this book is written as a call to action, although Pettifor profoundly disagrees with the monetary reform aims of the Positive Money movement. Her argument is that removing the banks' ability to create money would be unnecessarily restricting. She also notes that monetary reform has had its right-wing adherents. However, Pettifor's book shares the same critique of the power of banks to create money as debt. The failures of present financial arrangements are exposed and the same analogy is used for the over-exuberance of financial markets – the sorcerer's apprentice. The conclusion is less radical than the critique: the banks are to be tamed rather than the creation of money socialised as I propose in Chapter Seven of this book.

Zelizer, Viviane (1994) *The Social Meaning of Money*, Basic Books, New York.

Like Dodd, this is an early pioneering study that presents money as a social institution. Far from being a standardised mechanism of exchange or transfer, Zelizer sees people's approach and attitude to money as subverting that standardisation. She uses the concept of ear-marking to explore how people distinguish different sources of money and different uses of money. Sources of money may be honest (wages), dirty (crime) or unexpected (a lottery win). Money may be allocated in different ways. Wages may be put aside to pay bills, while an unexpected windfall may be spent. Domestically, attitudes to earning and spending may express differences such as seeing a wife's earnings as 'pin money'. Money given as a gift can be distinguished from welfare or charity. Zelizer notes that states are reluctant to give welfare payments as money, particularly in the US, preferring to distribute food stamps. As noted in Chapter Seven of this book, this attitude has only recently begun to change.

Further reading

Blyth, Mark (2013), *Austerity: The History of a Dangerous Idea*, **Oxford University Press, Oxford.**

While this is not a book about money, it is a book about myths and their power. It shows how austerity is politically and philosophically grounded. Blyth's book provides the ammunition to challenge contemporary assertion of the need for austerity.

Dodd, Nigel (2014) *The Social Life of Money*, **Princeton University Press, Princeton, NJ.**

In the first part of this book Dodd covers much of the same ground as is presented here: the origins of money, credit money and capitalism, financial failure, debt and austerity. However, Dodd's analysis of money is embedded in a dense theoretical framework drawing on classical and contemporary theory and philosophy that goes well beyond the discussion of the history and nature of money in this book. In the second part of his book Dodd introduces new aspects of money such as waste, territory, culture and utopia. Unlike many of the books in this list, *The Social Life of Money* is a theoretically expressive, rather than a campaigning, book.

Galbraith, John Kenneth (1975) *Money Whence it Came and Where it Went*, **Penguin, London.**

The economist John Kenneth Galbraith stands out in his exposure of the seeming sleight of hand by which money is created in the banking sector. He made the often-quoted statement 'the process by which banks create money is so simple the mind is repelled. Where something so important is involved, a deeper mystery seems only decent' (pp 18–19). Although somewhat dated in its policy context, this is a very readable book.

Huber, Joseph (2017) *Sovereign Money: Beyond Reserve Banking*, **Palgrave Macmillan, Basingstoke.**

Although the title of this book sounds rather technical, the author writes from the perspective of a sociologist. Huber shares the same analysis and proposals for monetary reform as Jackson and Dyson. He presents a critical history of money and banking and makes proposals to reclaim the sovereign power to create money from the banks. Theoretical debates and practical proposals are intertwined and theoretical differences are discussed, such as between currency theories (that money can be created through sovereign power) and banking theories (that money creation responds to 'bottom up' demand). Huber takes the side of the currency theorists. My argument here combines both sides of the argument by linking sovereign power to 'bottom up' participatory democracy as set out in Chapter Seven.

Ryan-Collins, Josh, Tony Greenham, Richard Werner and Andrew Jackson (2011) *Where Does Money Come From? A Guide to the UK Monetary and Banking System*, **New Economics Foundation, London.**

For anyone who wishes to have a short critical introduction to the present money and banking system together with radical proposals for reform.

Simmel, Georg (1907/1990) *The Philosophy of Money*, **Routledge, London.**

Simmel (1858–1918) was a German sociologist and philosopher who aimed at first to present a psychology of money. This broad cross-disciplinary approach makes this a complex book. Simmel was a contemporary of Knapp and Menger but he did not present such a specific view of the origin and nature of money. His book is in two parts. The first is a largely philosophical exploration of the nature of money. The second half is a more psychological and sociological analysis of the impact of money on individuals and society. He concludes that money brings freedom, but also rationalisation and objectification. Subjective value becomes subordinated to the blandness of monetary value. This reduces the quality and variety of human relationships to a colourless indifference. While this book is not an easy read, it is important as an early extensive exploration of money as a social institution.

Turner, Adair (2017) *Between Debt and the Devil: Money, Credit and Fixing Global Finance* **Princeton University Press, Princeton, NJ.**

At the time of the 2007–08 financial crisis Adair Turner was the newly appointed Chair of the UK Financial Services Authority, set up by the Labour government to monitor the financial sector. He therefore had a ringside seat to determine what went wrong. He acknowledges in his preface that, like most people, he didn't see the crisis coming. His book explores the background to the crisis, with particular emphasis on the role of private sector debt. His critique leads to some radical conclusions about the future of money and the role of banking.

Wolf, Martin (2014) *The Shifts and the Shocks: What We've Learned and Have Still to Learn from the Financial Crisis,* **Allen Lane, London.**

This is an interesting book by a leading *Financial Times* economist. Like Turner's book Wolf traces the causes and consequences of the 2007–08 financial crisis, concluding, that money creation cannot be left to the banking sector; rather, it should be treated as a public utility.

Wray, L. Randall (2012) *Modern Money Theory,* **Palgrave Macmillan, Basingstoke.**

This book is quite technical in that it aims to set out a practical alternative monetary theory. Modern money theory (MMT) shares the same critique of money and banking as the monetary reformers such as Jackson and Dyson (see above) but has a very different theoretical approach to the nature of money. The theoretical basis of MMT is presented by Wray in a final theoretical section of his book. The differences between the two movements, MMT and Monetary Reform, are explored in chapter 6 of my book *Debt or Democracy* (2015).

Wray, L. Randall (ed) (2004) *Credit and State Theories of Money: The Contribution of A. Mitchell Innes*, **Edward Elgar, Cheltenham.**

This is a collection of papers responding to the work of an early, but neglected, monetary theorist, Alfred Mitchell Innes (1864–1950). Mitchell Innes was a British diplomat who, while posted to Washington, wrote two prescient essays for a banking law journal, 'What is Money?' (1913) and 'The Credit Theory of Money' (1914). Perhaps because they were published in a legalistic journal the radical nature of his ideas was not recognised, although they were praised by Keynes. As the titles of the two articles suggest, Mitchell Innes put forward many of the radical ideas about money that have been relaunched in recent years. This collection was one of the early books on the new flowering of radical theories of money and contains essays by leading thinkers in the field.

Index